I0049276

How Smart People Think

Simple Frameworks for
Better Business Decisions

by
Dick Richardson

Copyright © 2025 by Dick Richardson
All rights reserved.

No part of this publication may be reproduced, stored in a retrieval
system, or transmitted in any form or by any means, electronic,
mechanical, photocopying, recording, scanning, or otherwise, without
the prior written permission of the author.

Limit of Liability/Disclaimer of Warranty:
Neither the publisher nor the author shall be liable for any loss of profit
or any other commercial damages, including but not limited to special,
incidental, consequential, personal, or other damages.

How Smart People Think
Simple Frameworks for Better Business Decisions
by Dick Richardson

1. BUS059000   BUSINESS & ECONOMICS / Skills
2. BUS007000   BUSINESS & ECONOMICS / Business Communication
/ General
3. SEL027000   SELF-HELP / Personal Growth / Success

ISBN (paperback): 979-8-88636-061-5
ISBN (ebook): 979-8-88636-062-2

Library of Congress Control Number: 2025917583

Cover design by Lewis Agrell

Printed in the United States of America

Authority Publishing
13389 Folsom Blvd #300-256
Folsom, CA 95630
800-877-1097
www.AuthorityPublishing.com

Dedication

Three people believed in this project
and encouraged me to write this book.

My wife Margaret "Mimi" Richardson
My friend Peter Z. Orton
My publisher Stephanie Chandler

Table of Contents

Foreword.   vii

Introduction.   ix

PART I: Foundations of Thinking   xiii

- Chapter 1: Map vs. Territory   1
- Chapter 2: Fast and Slow Thinking.   5
- Chapter 3: Circle of Control.   11

Part II: Avoiding Common Pitfalls.   17

- Chapter 4: Anchoring Bias   19
- Chapter 5: Confirmation Bias   25
- Chapter 6: Attribution Error   31
- Chapter 7: Sunk Cost   37
- Chapter 8: Loss Aversion   41
- Chapter 9: Marshmallows   45
- Chapter 10: Dr. Phil   51

Part III: Principles of Clarity   55

- Chapter 11: First Principles Thinking   57
- Chapter 12: Occam's Razor   61
- Chapter 13: Inversion   67
- Chapter 14: Six Honest Serving Men.   73
- Chapter 15: No-cost Consultant   79

Part IV: Decision Analysis Tools.   83

- Chapter 16: Divergent and Convergent Thinking. .   85
- Chapter 17: Pareto Principle.   91
- Chapter 18: Expected Value.   95
- Chapter 19: Opportunity Costs. 101
- Chapter 20: Second-Order Thinking. 107
- Chapter 21: Scenario Planning. 113
- Chapter 22: Probabilistic Thinking. 119

Part V: Dynamic Environments. 126

- Chapter 23: Say Three, Pick One. 127
- Chapter 24: OODA Loop. 131
- Chapter 25: Goal Shedding. 137
- Chapter 26: Eisenhower Matrix. 143
- Chapter 27: Bezos's Two-way Doors. 149
- Chapter 28: Zooming In and Out. 155
- Chapter 29: Tame and Wicked Problems. 161

Part VI: Personal Effectiveness. 166

- Chapter 30: Self-Efficacy. 167
- Chapter 31: Minimum Commitment. 171
- Chapter 32: Franklin Framework. 175
- Chapter 33: Anti-Fragility. 179
- Chapter 34: Bayesian Learning. 185
- Chapter 35: Stockdale Paradox. 189

Part VII: Weaving it all Together 193

- Chapter 36: The Latticework of Models. 195
- Chapter 37: Cruel Sea. 201
- Chapter 38: So What, Now What?. 207

Foreword

I knew it! At last, *How Smart People Think* confirms a suspicion I've long held.

Let me go back a bit. Dick Richardson has been a friend and mentor for more than thirty years, and he might be the most productive and innovative learning leader I've ever worked with.

And here's the thing: In all of those years of delivering brilliantly creative solutions at IBM and beyond, I never saw him break a sweat. He was always so relaxed. Solutions focused. Seemingly in command of the client and the process, immune to the chaos. He made it look easy. I started to suspect he must be harboring some kind of secret. What kind of shortcut was he taking?

It turns out that he was indeed taking shortcuts. But not the lazy kind; the smart kind.

With *How Smart People Think*, Dick has curated a treasure chest of "mental models" that brought actionable wisdom to his career. They will do the same for yours.

Imagine it: You're in one of those spiraling "blaming" conversations with your team, where someone is being scapegoated for some point of failure. Now imagine saying, "Hey guys, are we guilty of an Attribution Error here? What if we shifted our attention to the system rather than one person?" Boom. The energy changes. The emotional temperature changes. The problem-solving is back on track.

And all you did was invoke the model.

I can envision a world where leaders make a discipline of learning these mental models, just as we memorized our multiplication tables as kids. I believe this might be one of the few books that can actually raise your IQ.

How Smart People Think is arriving in the world at a good time. We are at the dawn of the AI revolution, and today there is a lot of speculation on whether AI is going to be our savior or our destroyer. Most of that fearful speculation is about a zombified generation seduced into outsourcing its ability to think to the robots.

That makes *How Smart People Think* a bit of a radical act. Maybe we call this "the resistance," because Dick is inviting us to recommit to our humanity by recommitting to thinking. And just as he's always done in his career in leadership development, he's equipping us with tools to do it. Smarter. Faster. More efficiently.

I was fortunate. Dick was a mentor to me when I was a young guy entering the organizational learning space. I absorbed a lot of these ideas by osmosis over a few decades of collaboration.

You're fortunate too, because you don't need twenty-five years. Just spend an afternoon with *How Smart People Think*, and you'll have the cheat code. The shortcuts. And then you'll be equipped to lead in a complex world that needs your best thinking more than ever before.

David Hutchens

Introduction
The Way You Think Shapes Your Life

You've launched your career. The first few years are exciting—new roles, new teams, new challenges. But they're also full of decisions that can change your trajectory: Should you take the promotion that pulls you into management? Should you stay with a stable company or jump to a start-up? Should you spend your evenings networking, upskilling, or protecting your work-life balance? These are not simple choices—and in today's fast-changing world, relying on "common sense" isn't enough.

In 2008, Brian Chesky was a young designer living in San Francisco, struggling to pay rent. Along with his co-founder Joe Gebbia, he came up with a scrappy idea: rent out air mattresses in their apartment to conference attendees when hotels were booked up. They called it "Airbed & Breakfast."

It didn't look promising. Friends told him it wasn't practical. Investors laughed them out of the room. To stay afloat, Chesky and Gebbia even sold custom cereal boxes during the election season ("Obama O's" and "Cap'n McCain's").

Then Chesky faced a career-defining decision. He received an offer for a stable design job. Or should he double down on a failing idea that no one believed in?

Here's where a mental model kicked in: **Opportunity Cost**. He realized the real cost of taking a job wasn't just about what he'd gain (a paycheck, stability), but what he would lose—the once-in-a-lifetime chance to build something that was his and that could change the way people travel.

Using the **Opportunity Cost** framework, Chesky chose to keep building Airbnb. That decision, made in his twenties when failure seemed almost certain, led to a company now valued in the tens of billions.

That's the power of mental models. They're lenses you use to see situations more clearly, frameworks that help you cut through complexity and make sharper choices. They don't give you answers, but they allow you to ask better questions.

The most successful leaders, entrepreneurs, and innovators use them constantly. In these pages you'll find the favorite decision-making models of smart people, including:

Warren Buffett	Richard Branson	Oprah Winfrey
Beyoncé	Vera Wang	Elon Musk
Steve Jobs	Sara Blakely	William Occam
Martha Stewart	Jamie Diamon	Jeff Bezos
Sully Sullenberger	Ekkapol Chantawong	

This book is your toolkit. Each chapter focuses on one mental model and is designed for action, with stories, real business examples, key takeaways, and applications.

The truth is that predictable progress is a thing of the past. Careers don't move in neat, upward lines anymore. They zigzag. They stall. They leap. But if you know how to think, you'll thrive no matter how the landscape shifts.

The way you think shapes the way you decide. And the way you decide shapes your career and life.

Let's get started.

PART I: Foundations of Thinking

Chapter 1
Map vs. Territory

The high-concept grocery chain, Harvest Mart, invested heavily in a new customer analytics system. The data (their "map") showed that customers most frequently bought milk, bread, and eggs, so the corporation moved those staples to the back of the store to "*increase dwell time.*"

Their spreadsheet said: *More walking = More impulse buys = More revenue.*

But in the **"territory"**—the real store—shoppers weren't playing along. In particular, busy parents and elderly customers hated the change and the extra walking. Complaints rose. Reviews fell. Cart abandonment increased.

Local store managers warned headquarters. But the corporate team trusted the data model. "It's working in our simulations," they insisted.

Within a year, sales declined across multiple locations. Only after visiting stores in person did the executives realize that the data map had missed real-world friction.

What is the problem?

People and organizations often mistake their assumptions, plans, data, or beliefs (the "map") for objective reality (the "territory"). Overreliance on mental and statistical maps can lead to dogmatic thinking and failure to see reality. This leads to misjudged risks, strategic blind spots, and subsequently poor decisions.

"The data showed what people bought—but not how they moved, felt, or reacted." – Harvest Mart spokesperson

What is the Map vs. Territory Mental Model?

The **Map vs. Territory** mental model reminds us that our models, theories, perceptions, and data are merely representations of reality, not reality itself. A "map" can be a business plan, forecast, org chart, customer persona, or even a belief system. The "territory" is what actually exists and unfolds in the real world.

A Real Business Example: White Star Line's RMS *Titanic*

In 1912, the RMS *Titanic* was marketed and believed to be **"unsinkable."** That belief—the map—was shared by the designers, owners, and even many passengers. The White Star Line had innovative watertight compartments, and it met or exceeded all safety regulations at the time.

Philip Franklin, Vice President of White Star, is quoted as saying, "We place absolute confidence in the *Titanic*. We believe the boat is unsinkable."

But the **territory**, the real-world physics of iceberg collisions, didn't care about reputations or engineering pride. When the ship struck an iceberg, it sank in under three hours, killing over 1,500 people. The discrepancy between the mental belief system of safety and the brutal reality was catastrophic.

Key Takeaways

- Reality always has the final say. No matter how elegant your model or strategy, you must continually compare it against the ground truth.
- Beware of belief traps. It's easy to confuse what you *want* to be true with what *is* true.
- Field feedback matters. Stay close to the front lines: customers, competitors, and data provide real-time updates to your map.

How to Apply the Map vs. Territory Mental Model

The **Map vs. Territory** mental model is about understanding that our perceptions, beliefs, and representations (the map) are simplifications or abstractions of reality (the territory). Effectively applying this model involves recognizing the gap between your assumptions or mental constructs and the actual state of affairs, which helps to avoid misjudgments.

Two simple steps:

First, clarify your assumptions (Your Map)

- List your beliefs, expectations, and mental models explicitly.
- Regularly question: "What assumptions am I making?"

Example:

At Amazon, the executives believed that the phone wait time for customer complaints was *"pretty good."*

Second, verify with real-world data (The Territory)

- Actively seek data or direct evidence to challenge or confirm your assumptions.
- Ask: "Is my belief aligned with real-world evidence?"

For example:

During a staff meeting at Amazon, the discussion shifted to complaints about wait times for calls to customer service. The head of operations informed everyone that the issue had been resolved. Jeff Bezos called the customer complaint line on the speakerphone. The hold time extended to nearly ten minutes, changing the dynamics of the meeting.

Related Frameworks

- Confirmation Bias or the tendency to seek information that confirms existing beliefs can create false maps in our minds.
- First Principles Thinking is the process of breaking problems down into fundamental truths and reasoning up from there, instead of relying on assumptions. This is an excellent way of verifying our maps.
- Thinking backward from the desired outcome or focusing on avoiding failure through Inversion thinking can help us create new and more accurate mental maps.
- Seeking the perspectives of others by using the No-cost Consultant model is an informal way to test our assumptions.

"The map is not the territory, but if correct, it has a similar structure to the territory, which accounts for its usefulness." – *Alfred Korzybski*

Chapter 2
Fast and Slow Thinking

On July 3, 1988, the USS Vincennes, a US Navy cruiser in the Persian Gulf, mistakenly identified an Iranian civilian airliner (Iran Air Flight 655) as an attacking fighter jet. Under battlefield pressure, it shot it down, resulting in the deaths of all 290 civilians on board.

The ship's crew was operating in a combat zone, under high stress and uncertainty. Multiple cognitive biases—**Confirmation bias, Anchoring**, and **Pattern matching**—kicked in. The crew misread the aircraft's transponder signals and ignored conflicting data. Rapid, fear-based decision-making using incomplete data resulted in a catastrophic error.

Despite advanced technology and trained personnel, the high-pressure environment triggered quick, instinctive reactions rather than slower, structured analysis. The radar profile didn't correspond to any enemy aircraft. The aircraft was climbing, not descending like an attacker, and none of the crew double-checked the electronic identification markers.

A formal investigation later revealed that the incorrect assumptions could have been contested with better deliberation.

What is the problem?

We humans often make quick, emotionally driven decisions through automatic thinking.

While this can be advantageous at times, it may also lead to cognitive biases and judgment errors—especially in complex, high-stakes, or unfamiliar situations where deliberate reasoning is required. Some symptoms of the problem include:

- Snap decisions based on limited data
- Failure to analyze second-order effects or long-term consequences
- Overreaction to short-term signals (e.g., fear, trends, peer pressure)

"When you're in a rush, you tend to believe what you want to believe." – *Charlie Munger*

What is the Thinking Fast and Thinking Slow Mental Model?

The Thinking Fast and Thinking Slow mental model refers to the dual-system theory of cognition proposed by psychologist Daniel Kahneman. It describes how humans engage in two modes of thinking:

- System 1: Fast, intuitive, automatic, and emotional
- System 2: Slow, deliberate, logical, and effortful

This model helps explain why people often make quick judgments that may be biased or flawed, and how deliberate reasoning can override those errors. In academic circles, this is known as the "Dual-Process Theory."

The model is valuable because it helps you identify when you are thinking too quickly and need to slow down. It provides a framework to toggle between intuitive and analytical thinking, and it encourages metacognition: thinking about how we think.

A Real Business Example: Target's Failed Expansion into Canada (2013–2015)

In 2013, the US department store Target launched a rapid expansion into Canada, opening 124 stores in just one year. This aggressive rollout was driven by enthusiasm and confidence stemming from its success in the United States. Target's CEO, Gregg Steinhafel, was the architect of the Canadian expansion. He said, "We're successful in the US, so we'll succeed in Canada." His overconfidence and pattern-matching bias led to hasty decisions: skipping full pilots, rushing logistics, and underestimating market differences. This flawed decision-making resulted in $5.4 billion in losses.

The chart below illustrates how Target used System 1 thinking and how they could have used System 2 thinking.

Decision Area	System 1: What Target Did (Fast Thinking)	System 2: What Target Could Have Done (Slow Thinking)
Expansion Speed	Launched 124 stores in 1 year—rapid, large-scale rollout	Begin with a pilot program in select regions; test and iterate before scaling
Assumptions	Assumed US success model would work identically in Canada	Conducted deep market research to identify local expectations, supply chain needs, and consumer preferences
Supply Chain	Overestimated readiness—poor logistics led to empty shelves	Stress-test infrastructure and vendor readiness through phased inventory simulations
Pricing Strategy	Kept US-style pricing, which appeared expensive after currency conversion and import costs	Adjust pricing models to local market conditions and tax structures
Store Experience	Focused on brand recognition and footprint, not experience	Invest in customer insight studies to learn shopping behaviors, cultural nuances, and expectations
Feedback Mechanism	No meaningful learning loop—too fast to course correct	Built in deliberate checkpoints to monitor early store performance and adjust strategy dynamically
Mindset	Confident, reactive, expansion-first mindset	Cautious, reflective, feedback-driven approach with scenario planning

Key Takeaways

- Use fast thinking for routine or time-sensitive decisions, but don't rely on it for strategy, hiring, or innovation.
- Biases tend to reside in System 1: confirmation bias, halo effect, and anchoring often emerge in snap judgments.
- Train yourself to trigger System 2 thinking in high-stakes decisions: pause, reflect, ask "What am I missing?"
- People and organizations need rituals for slowing down: checklists, **Premortems**, and using the **No-cost Consultant** can prompt analytical processing.

How to Apply The Thinking Fast and Thinking Slow Mental Model

First, you need to know the two systems.

System 1 is fast, intuitive, emotional, and often automatic. It's effective for time-sensitive, routine, low-risk decisions.

System 2 is slower, rational, and deliberate. It's best for complex, unfamiliar, strategic, or high-stakes decisions.

Second, you should establish mental cues to help evaluate your thinking. One way to do this is to train yourself to ask, "Am I making this decision too quickly?" Another meaningful approach is to listen to your body and emotions. Are there any uneasy feelings or mild anxiety about your decision?

Third, use tools that promote slow thinking.

- **Premortems** can help you anticipate potential failures. "Imagine this decision failed a year from now. Why did it fail?"
- Use the **No-cost Consultant** framework to check your thinking.
- Use **Scenario Planning** to map out possible futures before making a commitment.

These tools relieve your brain of the burden and create external structures to activate System 2.

Related Frameworks

- We can fool ourselves with **Confirmation Bias** because we all have a tendency to seek information that confirms existing beliefs.
- **Divergent and Convergent Thinking** is a process that not only slows our thinking but also gives us a structure for the problem-solving process. One way to check your thinking is the **Dr. Phil Mental Model**—using reflective accountability.
- **Inversion Thinking** is one of the most effective System 2 processes for avoiding mistakes and failure.

"System 1 is the first draft. System 2 is the editor." – *Unknown*

Chapter 3
Circle of Control

During the summer of 2018, Ekkapol Chantawong, also known as Coach Ek, led his Wild Boars soccer team on a short trip into Thailand's Tham Luang cave system. Unfortunately, heavy rains flooded the caves and trapped Coach Ek and his twelve players deep inside. In the darkness and uncertainty, Coach Ek faced a difficult situation: He didn't know why the water was rising, when they would be rescued, or how long their oxygen supply would last.

Despite these overwhelming circumstances, Coach Ek remained focused on what he could control to keep himself and the boys safe, calm, and alive for the next eighteen days until they were finally rescued.

With a positive attitude and using techniques he learned as a former monk, Coach Ek taught the boys meditation to help them stay calm, conserve energy, and manage their fear and anxiety. He also made sure that everyone received equal portions of the limited food supplies brought by the team. He even sacrificed his own share to prioritize the boys' survival. Throughout this ordeal, Coach Ek emphasized the importance of sticking together and supporting one another.

After nine days, rescuers finally found all thirteen individuals alive—a testament to Coach Ek's determination to focus on what he could control. His ability to maintain his and his team's mental and physical well-being gave them precious time while rescuers devised an unprecedented extraction plan. All were eventually rescued.

What is the problem?

We can become distracted by issues or concerns over which we have no influence. Any ergs of energy we spend on those things are wasted. Instead, successful people focus on the things that they can influence. Sometimes it's hard to tell the difference.

"God grant me the serenity to accept the things I cannot change, courage to change the things I can, and wisdom to know the difference." – *Reinhold Niebuhr*

What is the Circle of Control Mental Model?

The **Circle of Control** mental model is a valuable tool for focusing your energy on things you can directly influence, rather than worrying about matters outside your control. The framework categorizes concern into three categories:

- **Circle of Control**: Things within your power to affect, such as actions, choices, and reactions.
- **Circle of Influence**: Things you can impact but not fully control, like team dynamics or client decisions.
- **Circle of Concern**: Things you have no control over, such as market trends or economic downturns.

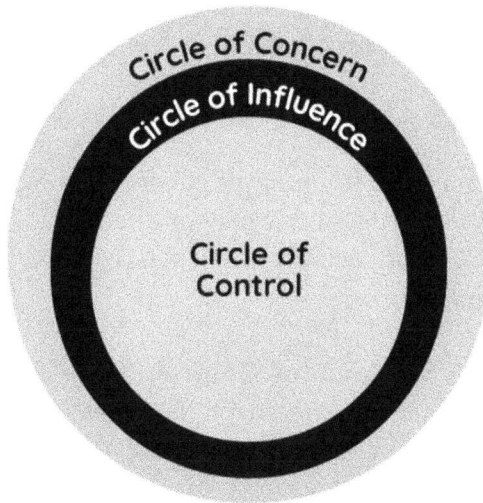

As a professional, you should focus on the factors you can control or at least influence. Worrying about things beyond your control provides no benefit. By concentrating on the two inner circles, you can alleviate stress for yourself and your employees, enhance productivity, and achieve meaningful progress.

A Real Business Example: Starbucks Facing COVID

Starbucks' core business is to bring people together through food and drinks. However, the COVID-19 pandemic posed a threat to this mission and could have spelled disaster for the company. CEO Kevin Johnson and his team recognized that many external factors were beyond their control, so they shifted their focus toward what they could control and influence.

What They Could Control and Influence:

- Employee Safety: Implementing stricter health protocols to keep employees safe.
- Customer Engagement: Expanding mobile ordering and contactless payment options.

- Community Support: Providing free coffee to healthcare workers to foster goodwill.

What Was Outside Their Control:

- Length of the pandemic or government mandates.
- Changes in customer behavior due to fear.
- Government actions to curtail travel and people congregating.

By prioritizing its **Circle of Control**, Starbucks managed to maintain customer loyalty, adapt its operations, and emerge stronger after the pandemic. The most important takeaways from this approach include:

- Investing energy into what is achievable leads to progress even in difficult circumstances.
- Avoiding wasted efforts on uncontrollable factors minimizes frustration and inefficiency.
- Empowering others within their circle encourages proactive and solution-based thinking.
- Adapting to the situation fosters resilience and innovative solutions during times of crisis.

Key Takeaways

Understanding the amount of influence you do or don't have guides your decision-making.

- Husbanding your resources. By mapping what's in your control vs. what isn't, you avoid wasting time on the unchangeable. This will reduce stress.
- Action planning. This framework helps you prioritize your efforts to where they will have the greatest impact.
- Proactive people expand their **Circle of Influence** by mastering their **Circle of Control**: becoming trusted,

capable, and consistent. Reactive people shrink their influence by obsessing over their **Circle of Concern**, which creates anxiety and drains agency.

How to Apply the Circle of Control Mental Model

Reframe complaints into control. When you catch yourself or others complaining, ask:

"What part of this is within my control?" For example, turn "This client is impossible" into "I can control how I prepare and communicate."

Complaining actually trains our brains to feel helpless. Reframing builds power.

Apply it during uncertainty. When the world feels overwhelming (layoffs, family stress, etc.), pause and name three things you *can* control right now. This creates a grounded "reset" moment.

Use it in coaching and other conversations. When mentoring, coaching, or managing, ask:

- "Which part of this can I control?"
- "What's in my influence that I haven't tapped into yet?"

This can foster clarity, ownership, and emotional regulation in others.

When using this model, do it as a group. Draw three concentric circles on a chart and ask your team to identify what we control, influence, and what we can't affect. Model the process and then step back to allow the team to perform the analysis. Engaging in this activity as a group involves them and enhances their understanding of their roles. The chart serves as a visual representation of our abilities and limitations.

Related Frameworks

- **Tame and Wicked Problems**: Complicated vs. complex problems need different solutions. The more wicked the problem, the less control you may have.
- Understanding **Reciprocity** and leveraging the human tendency to return favors can increase your circle of influence.

"Make the best use of what is in your power, and take the rest as it happens." – *Epictetus*

Part II: Avoiding Common Pitfalls

Chapter 4
Anchoring Bias

In 1993, Williams-Sonoma introduced a $275 bread maker that did not sell well. Surveys revealed that customers perceived it as too expensive. So, the company tried something counterintuitive: they introduced a second bread maker priced at $429, a more advanced model with just a few added features.

The result? Sales of the original $275 bread maker spiked.

What is the problem?

People often make skewed decisions because they unconsciously fixate on initial information (the anchor), even when it is arbitrary, irrelevant, or misleading. This can lead to flawed judgments. Some common examples include:

- Price distortion occurs when customers overvalue or undervalue a product based on the first number they encounter (original price, decoy pricing).

- Negotiation traps: Initial offers have a significant impact on final outcomes, even when they are unrealistic.
- Forecasting errors: Initial estimates anchor expectations, causing teams to under-adjust when new data emerges.
- Hiring misjudgments: Early impressions (resume prestige, past salary) can skew the evaluation of actual skills or fit.

People don't evaluate values in isolation. They compare. Anchoring sets the mental baseline, often nudging decisions without your awareness.

"We tend to give disproportionate weight to the first piece of information we receive." – Chip Heath & Dan Heath, *Decisive: How to Make Better Choices in Life and Work*

What is the Anchoring Bias Mental Model?

Anchoring bias is a cognitive bias where individuals rely too heavily on the first piece of information (the "anchor") they receive when making decisions. Once an anchor is set, it shapes and skews all subsequent judgments, even when the anchor is arbitrary or irrelevant.

In business, this often distorts pricing, forecasting, salary negotiations, and strategic planning.

You can use **Anchoring Bias** to influence others, and others may be using it to prejudice your thinking.

A Real Business Example: JCPenney's "Fair and Square" Pricing

In 2011, JCPenney hired Apple executive Ron Johnson to revamp the struggling retailer. One of his big ideas: eliminate sales and markdowns in favor of *"everyday low prices."*

However, customers of Penny's were used to promotional

sales. Shoppers were anchored to the original high price and accustomed to deep discounts (e.g., "$60 shirt—50% off!"). Johnson's new strategy removed that anchor. Suddenly, a $30 shirt without a markdown *felt* like a bad deal, even though it was the same price.

Sales plunged. Customers didn't feel like they were getting a bargain, even when the price was fair. Within a year, Johnson was fired, and the company returned to its old pricing model.

Key Takeaways

- First impressions stick: The initial price, number, or message can anchor perception—intentionally or not.
- Anchors can be artificial: Even irrelevant numbers or arbitrary information can skew decisions.
- Re-anchoring is hard: Once consumers or stakeholders are conditioned to expect a particular baseline, shifting it is risky and slow.

How to Apply the Anchoring Bias Mental Model

There are two ways to apply the Anchoring Bias mental model:

1. Recognize whether you're falling prey to the bias
2. Use anchoring to influence others

Recognizing the anchor

Train yourself to identify the *first anchor* in any decision conversation.

- Ask: "What is the first number, idea, or impression I've been given?"
- Example: In a meeting, someone says, "This project should take three months." That becomes the unconscious benchmark—even if it's flawed.

Scrub away arbitrary anchors when evaluating alternatives.

- Ask yourself: "Where did this number come from?" "Is it relevant and accurate or is it just the first thing I saw/heard?"
- Try to find objective benchmarks or comparisons (industry data, historical performance) to counteract emotional or irrelevant anchors.

Using the anchor

Deliberately set an anchor to influence others.

- Start a negotiation or conversation with a value to set a baseline perception in the other person's mind.
- Example: When launching a new product, introduce a higher-priced version first to make the core offering feel like a deal (see: Williams-Sonoma bread maker).

In either case, we recommend you pause before making decisions to consider whether anchors are in play. **Anchoring Bias** is fast and intuitive. Slowing down helps override it.

Related Frameworks

- You should also be aware of **Confirmation Bias**, which is the tendency to seek information that confirms existing beliefs. Both can skew your judgment.
- One way to mitigate **Anchoring Bias** is by using the **Expected Value** mental model. This model allows you to multiply the outcome value by its probability.
- A good way to counteract any bias is by using **First Principles Thinking**, which is breaking problems down into fundamental truths and reasoning up from there, instead of relying on assumptions.

"The first number put on the table strongly shapes how people think—even when it's completely arbitrary." – *Daniel Kahneman, Nobel Laureate in Behavioral Economics*

Chapter 5
Confirmation Bias

In 1989, a violent assault in New York City's Central Park led to the arrest of five teenagers, later known as the Central Park Five. The police and prosecutors, convinced of the teenagers' guilt, focused on obtaining confessions instead of investigating other leads. The authorities interpreted evidence through the lens of their belief in the teenagers' guilt.

Inconsistent and contradictory confessions were seen as supporting the case, while the lack of physical evidence connecting the boys to the crime was overlooked. This confirmation bias fueled the investigation, disregarding signs that indicated other possibilities.

Years later, DNA evidence and a confession from the real perpetrator, Matias Reyes, exonerated the Central Park Five. The case became a powerful example of how confirmation bias can have devastating consequences, as the authorities' unwavering belief in their initial theory led to wrongful convictions and ruined lives.

What is the problem?

We humans have an innate need to find consistency in our beliefs. Our brains often use shortcuts, or heuristics, to quickly make sense of information. As a result, we more readily seek evidence that supports our existing beliefs rather than critically evaluating all possible perspectives. This can lead to poor decisions.

"A man hears what he wants to hear and disregards the rest." – *Paul Simon, The Boxer*

What is the Confirmation Bias Mental Model?

Confirmation bias is a cognitive tendency to seek, interpret, and remember information that supports one's existing beliefs while disregarding or undervaluing evidence that contradicts them. Although this mental shortcut can simplify complex decision-making, it often leads to flawed judgments and reinforces preexisting misconceptions or biases. This bias arises from a desire for consistency and the emotional comfort of affirming one's worldview.

Those who are influenced by confirmation bias tend to:

- Give more weight to evidence that supports their beliefs.
- Disregard or reject evidence that goes against their beliefs.
- Interpret ambiguous information in ways that confirm their viewpoints.
- Fail to look at information that contraindicates their assumptions.

This bias is widespread. It can influence political views, personal decisions, and even scientific research as evidenced by our example.

A Real Business Example: Elizabeth Holmes and Theranos

Elizabeth Holmes, the mastermind behind Theranos, is a perfect example of confirmation bias in the world of entrepreneurship. Initially, Holmes genuinely believed in her idea to create a revolutionary medical technology that would replace traditional, time-consuming testing methods. She was convinced that Theranos' compact device, capable of running hundreds of medical tests with just a few drops of blood, would change the landscape of healthcare. However, this strong belief led her to focus only on information that supported her vision while disregarding crucial evidence that proved the technology was not viable.

How Confirmation Bias Can Influence Decisions:

- Selective attention to positive feedback: Holmes actively sought out investors and partners who shared her enthusiasm and downplayed any technical issues with the device.
- Dismissal of negative evidence: Despite reports and feedback from engineers and scientists within Theranos raising red flags about the technology's flaws, Holmes chose to ignore or brush them off, remaining firm in her belief that breakthroughs were imminent.

Reinforcement through Echo Chambers:

To further reinforce her beliefs, Holmes surrounded herself with influential individuals who lacked technical expertise and could not challenge her claims.

Unfortunately, this confirmation bias ultimately led Holmes to continue promoting and raising funds for Theranos, even as evidence mounted against its success. The truth was eventually revealed, resulting in the company's downfall. In January 2022, Holmes was convicted of defrauding investors and sentenced to eleven years in prison.

It's important to examine the investors in Theranos. Despite her lack of concrete evidence, Holmes managed to persuade highly intelligent individuals to invest. Among these prominent names were Henry Kissinger, George Shultz, James Mattis, Rupert Murdoch, and Walmart's Walton family, who collectively invested $150 million in the company.

These influential figures were likely also affected by cognitive bias, which can cloud judgment and lead to poor decisions. In contrast, more traditional healthcare venture capitalists chose not to invest in Theranos because they actively sought ways to challenge their own biases. For instance, they pointed out the absence of published, peer-reviewed clinical research on Theranos' technology.

Key Takeaways

- We see what we expect to see. It's a natural brain tendency, not a personal flaw, but it can lead to flawed thinking, poor decisions, and closed-mindedness.
- Intelligence doesn't immunize you. Being intelligent makes you better at rationalizing, not always better at reasoning.
- It affects all areas of your life:
  - In leadership: You might favor employees who echo your views, missing out on real innovation.
  - In relationships: You could misinterpret actions to fit your assumptions about someone.
  - In news consumption: You gravitate toward sources that reinforce your worldview.

How to Apply the Confirmation Bias Mental Model

It's hard to counteract your own **Confirmation Bias**. That said, there are two actions you can take.

- Deliberately seek disconfirming evidence. If you daily consume news outlets, select a wide range of political sites and you may recognize bias. On some outlets, a group may be called "terrorists" or "insurgents," whereas on others the same group is called "freedom fighters" or "protestors."
- Check your knowledge and beliefs by asking good questions:
  - o "How do I know this to be true?"
  - o "What would prove me wrong?"
  - o Invert the question: "If the opposite were true, what would I expect to see?"
  - o "Is this a belief or a fact?"

Related Frameworks

- **Occam's Razor** – The simplest definition of the problem and of the solution is often true.
- Understanding the **Social Proof** mental model can help you recognize the influence of others' thoughts and behavior may be skewing your opinion.

"The first principle is that you must not fool yourself, as you are the easiest person to fool." – *Richard Feynman*

Chapter 6
Attribution Error

A Southwest Airlines flight attendant was rude to several passengers on a crowded flight. Passengers complained to the airline via text, email, and letter. Initially, executives considered punishing or even firing the flight attendant for having a "bad attitude."

But Herb Kelleher, the legendary CEO, paused and asked more profound questions:

- "Was the flight attendant dealing with unusual stress?"
- "Did she have personal problems that she was dealing with?"
- "What was the work environment like that day?"
- "Was this part of a broader pattern or an isolated case?"

An investigation revealed that the flight attendant was not dealing with any personal issues that could affect her performance. The crew of that aircraft had worked a double shift due to weather delays. The airline's new scheduling system had glitches, forcing crews into extreme overtime. The employee hadn't eaten or rested for over twelve hours.

Kelleher's response: Instead of firing her, Southwest fixed the scheduling systems and ensured that crews had mandatory rest breaks. This story moved through Southwest's rumor mill very quickly. Employee morale rose, customer service scores improved, and Southwest avoided a wrongful termination lawsuit by recognizing that the real issue wasn't the person but the system.

What is the problem?

Attribution Error is a mental mistake in which you incorrectly explain someone's behavior by blaming their character, personality, or intentions while overlooking the influence of potential external factors, circumstances, or the environment.

"We judge others by their actions, but ourselves by our intentions."
– *Anonymous*

What is the Attribution Error Mental Model?

The **Attribution Error** mental model explains how and why people systematically misinterpret the causes of others' behavior. Instead of accurately considering external circumstances, we blame people's character, abilities, or motives.

You see this error in two different ways:

- In others. When viewing others, we overestimate personality-based explanations for others' actions and underestimate situational explanations. "He missed the deadline because he's disorganized."
- In ourselves. When viewing ourselves, we make the opposite error. We credit ourselves when things go well ("I'm smart!") and blame outside forces when things go

badly ("I missed the deadline because my daughter was sick. It wasn't my fault!").

Humans often default to this approach because it is quicker and simpler than analyzing complex situational factors. However, this mental shortcut in leadership, decision-making, and business frequently results in costly misjudgments.

A Real Business Example: The Kodak Collapse

In the 1990s, Kodak's leadership was often personally blamed for the company's collapse into bankruptcy. Critics said Kodak's executives were foolish, arrogant, and resistant to change—a classic attribution to character flaws.

In reality, this was a very complex situation. While leadership mistakes occurred, massive external forces were at play, including:

- Rapid emergence of digital photography
- Market disruption from cheaper international competitors
- Shifting consumer behavior away from print photography
- Technological lock-in and inertia within the giant corporation by middle management

Kodak's leaders didn't fail purely because of personal ineptitude or stubbornness. They were also caught amid significant systemic and technological shifts with which many companies struggled. Consider other companies that faced the same criticism of their leadership.

Company	What Happened	Parallel to Kodak
Blockbuster	Ignored the rise of digital streaming (Netflix, YouTube) and clung to physical rentals. Filed for bankruptcy in 2010.	Technology shift underestimated; leadership blamed for "arrogance" rather than recognizing market inevitability.
BlackBerry (RIM)	Failed to respond fast enough to smartphones' evolution (iPhone, Android). Market share collapsed after 2007.	Blamed leaders for stubbornness —but larger shift was touchscreen-based ecosystems beyond their control.
Borders Books	Outsourced online sales to Amazon instead of building their own platform. Collapsed in 2011.	Leadership scapegoated, but underlying e-commerce tsunami was devastating for most traditional retailers.
Myspace	Early dominance in social networking but failed to innovate against Facebook's superior user experience. Sold at a massive loss in 2011.	Easy to blame management—but the social internet changed radically faster than anyone predicted.
Yahoo!	Missed major acquisition opportunities (Google, Facebook) and lost its dominance in search and content. Decline throughout 2000s.	Public blamed poor executive decisions— but the competition and ad market transformed the terrain.

Judging others—whether leaders or employees—solely based on outcomes, without appreciating the situation, often leads organizations to scapegoat individuals instead of addressing real systemic problems.

Key Takeaways

- People are not always the problem. We instinctively blame individuals, but often the real cause is situational: systems, incentives, stressors, or environments.
- Quick judgments lead to wrong solutions. When we label people too fast ("lazy," "incompetent"), we waste time fixing symptoms instead of fixing root causes.
- Self-awareness protects your leadership. Leaders who recognize their own attribution errors make wiser decisions, build stronger teams, and avoid unnecessary conflict.

How to Apply the Attribution Bias Mental Model

To mitigate attribution bias, you need to focus on three things:

1. Separate the people from the problem. When evaluating performance, ask: "What external pressures or factors shaped this behavior?"
2. Slow down. Quick labeling ("they're lazy," "they're arrogant") blinds you to deeper causes you could address.
3. Train yourself and other leaders in situational thinking. Strong leadership cultures consistently teach managers to ask: "What context produced this result?" not just "Who caused this?"

Related Frameworks

- Confirmation Bias is our tendency to seek information that confirms our existing beliefs and to disregard or

counter anything that contradicts them.
- If you fall prey to Attribution Bias, you are likely to pursue information that reaffirms your mistaken beliefs.
- Using the Six Honest Serving Men model will help you look at facts rather than assumptions.

"Never attribute to malice that can be explained by circumstance."
– *Hanlon's Razor*

Chapter 7
Sunk Cost

In the 1960s, the British and French governments jointly funded the Concorde project—a cutting-edge supersonic passenger jet. As costs spiraled far beyond original estimates and demand projections weakened, it became increasingly clear that the aircraft would never be commercially viable.

Yet both governments continued to invest in the project, partly because they had already invested hundreds of millions of dollars. Politicians and executives justified continued funding with variations of "We've come too far to quit now."

Concorde was a financial failure. Only fourteen jets were ever put into service. None made a profit. The fiasco was so bad that a new term was coined: *Concorde fallacy*. The Cambridge Dictionary defines the Concorde fallacy as: "The idea that you should continue to spend money on a project, product, etc., in order not to waste the money or effort you have already put into it, which may lead to bad decisions."

What is the problem?

Humans often make irrational decisions by allowing past, unrecoverable investments (sunk costs) to influence current and future choices, even when those investments have no bearing on future outcomes.

The problem lies in how people let emotional attachment, ego, and fear of waste distort their judgment. Instead of asking, "What's the best decision from this point forward?" they ask, "How can I justify what I've already spent?"

This faulty thinking can manifest itself in many ways:

- Staying in failing ventures or relationships
- Throwing good money after bad
- Wasting time and resources trying to "make it work"

"Never ask a barber if you need a haircut. And never ask someone who sunk costs into a project if it should continue." – *Nassim Nicholas Taleb*

What is the Sunk Cost Mental Model?

The sunk cost fallacy is a cognitive bias where individuals continue investing in a losing endeavor because they have already committed resources (time, money, effort) that cannot be recovered. The Sunk Cost Framework is a rational decision-making model that asserts decisions should be based on future value and outcomes, not on past unrecoverable investments.

A Real Business Example: SuccessBreaks

In 2021, my son and I started a YouTube channel—SuccessBreaks. The purpose of the channel was "To provide entrepreneurs with short and concise videos on topics that matter, such as entrepreneurship, sales, marketing, personal development, and more."

We purchased the domain name, bought recording equipment, and hired a videographer. We enjoyed making videos together; it was fun. However, we wanted this endeavor to be successful and beneficial for entrepreneurs. We set a checkpoint for one year, and when that time came, we sat down to assess our work. We had failed. We hadn't met our objectives for subscribers or page views, and we incurred financial costs that we couldn't recover. But the greater sunk costs were our efforts and ego. We wished to make those emotional investments meaningful. Admitting failure was hard, but we decided to stop making SuccessBreaks videos, which wasn't easy.

Key Takeaways

- You should ignore unrecoverable costs. Only future costs and benefits should influence your decisions. Unrecoverable expenditures are not relevant.
- Rational abandonment should not be perceived as failure. Quitting a losing venture isn't a sign of weakness—it's a sign of strategic discipline.
- Escalation of commitment is risky. The more you've invested, the harder it becomes psychologically to walk away. That is emotional and not logical.

How to Apply the Sunk Cost Mental Model

Here are the basic steps to avoid the sunk cost fallacy.

1. Ask the golden question: "If I hadn't already spent this time/money/effort, would I make the same decision today?" You're likely caught in a sunk cost trap if the answer is no.
2. Identify the sunk costs: List what cannot be recovered— money already spent, time and energy invested, and emotional or reputational costs. Then cross them out, because they are irrelevant to future decisions.

3. Evaluate your current options objectively: Focus on projected future costs, expected future benefits, and any opportunity costs of continuing vs. stopping.
4. Watch for emotional red flags, such as: "I don't want to waste what I've already done." "I need to justify my past decisions." "Quitting makes me look bad." These are emotional biases—not business logic.
5. Create pre-set checkpoints or tripwires. Before starting a new project, define success/failure thresholds and schedule decision checkpoints. You can even establish an objective advisor or "red team" to review progress.

Remind yourself often that what's lost is gone. "What I choose now is what matters."

Related Frameworks

- The **Loss Aversion** mental model can help you understand the human tendency to fear losses even more than they value equivalent gains.
- **Opportunity Costs** should be considered when evaluating **Sunk Costs**.
- The **Dr. Phil** mental model can help you make better decisions when sunk costs are involved by anticipating how you will feel in the future if losses continue.
- **Scenario Planning** involves preparing for various potential futures. This can help you release previous investments of time and money.

"When you find yourself in a hole, stop digging." – *Will Rogers*

Chapter 8
Loss Aversion

One of the most famous stories illustrating how we value things comes from research conducted by Daniel Kahneman and Amos Tversky. In the experiment, participants received a coffee mug as a gift. Afterwards, they were asked if they would sell it and, if so, at what price. Another group of participants, who did not receive a mug, was asked how much they would be willing to pay for one of the mugs.

The results showed that those who owned the mug valued it significantly higher (an average of $7) compared to those who were willing to purchase it (an average of $3).

This illustrates **Loss Aversion**, where people value something more once they take ownership of it. This makes it harder for them to let go and creates a sense of "loss" even if they just acquired the item.

What is the problem?

Because losses feel twice as painful as equivalent gains feel pleasurable, people often:

- Avoid smart risks
- Say no to innovation or bold moves
- Overvalue short-term losses over long-term gains

Example: An investor avoids a promising startup because of the fear of losing capital, even though the upside potential is significant.

It also reinforces the "sunk cost fallacy." Because we hate experiencing losses, we often double down on bad decisions, thinking:

- "I've already put too much into this to quit now."
- "Maybe it'll turn around."

Example: A business keeps funding a failing product to avoid admitting a loss, wasting more resources in the process.

What is the Loss Aversion Mental Model?

Loss Aversion is a concept in behavioral economics that explains how people tend to prioritize avoiding losses over acquiring equivalent gains. In simpler terms, we are more affected by the pain of losing something than by the pleasure of gaining it. This is why individuals are much more emotionally impacted by a loss of, say, $50,000 in their stock portfolio than by a gain of $50,000.

You can guard against making poor decisions by being aware of this psychological tendency.

A Real Business Example: How Netflix Retains Subscribers

Netflix has consistently used **Loss Aversion** to enhance customer retention. They invest heavily in personalized recommendations and exclusive content to make subscribers feel as though they would be losing something valuable if they were to cancel their subscriptions. By playing on the fear of missing out on content tailored specifically for them, it becomes increasingly difficult to leave.

Netflix also strategically uses features like "Continue Watching" to keep users engaged and remind them of the value they could potentially lose if they unsubscribe.

Key Takeaways

- People fear losses more than gains.
- Framing is important: Focusing on what customers could lose (like exclusivity, discounts, or personalization) can be more effective than emphasizing potential gains.
- Emotions drive decisions: Loss Aversion triggers emotional decision-making. That means that you can build stronger customer loyalty by tapping into these emotions.

How to Apply the Loss Aversion Mental Model

Two ways to apply the Loss Aversion Framework: (1) to check your thinking and (2) as a way to influence others.

To check your thinking by recognizing when loss aversion is at play, ask yourself:

- "Am I avoiding this action because I fear losing something (time, money, reputation)?"
- "Is the pain of potential loss truly outweighing the probability or size of gain?"

Be aware: **Loss Aversion** can lead to overvaluing current assets or sunk costs. To rebalance:

- Focus on future value, not past effort.
- Set thresholds for when to cut losses.

- Use external feedback to check your bias.

To influence others, reframe decisions in terms of potential losses. That is, frame in terms of what's at stake if they *don't* act, not just what they might gain.

For example, instead of saying: "You'll save $200/year with this service," say: "You're losing $200 every year by not switching."

Loss Aversion is a powerful technique in sales, marketing, leadership, and personal motivation.

Related Frameworks

- Other people may not share your aversion to loss. That's why the **No-cost Consultant** model of seeking perspectives from others before making decisions can help you make choices with greater clarity.
- Honestly, considering how you might feel about a decision in the future could offer insight into **Loss Aversion**. The **Dr. Phil** mental model achieves this perfectly.

"People are not afraid of change. They fear loss." – *John P. Kotter*

Chapter 9
Marshmallows

The marshmallow experiment was a well-known psychology study conducted by Walter Mischel at Stanford University during the late 1960s and early 1970s. It examined young children's ability to delay gratification, revealing significant insights about future success.

The experiment:

- Children (four to five years old) each sat alone in a room in front of a single marshmallow on a table.
- They were told: "If you don't eat the marshmallow while I'm gone, you'll get a second one when I return."
- The researcher left the room for fifteen minutes.
- Some kids quickly ate the marshmallow. Others struggled—fidgeted, sang, covered their eyes—but resisted temptation and earned the second marshmallow.

Years later, follow-up studies tracked the children's progress. Those children who waited and received the second marshmallow:

- Had higher SAT scores
- Had better emotional coping skills
- Had lower rates of obesity, substance abuse, and even divorce
- Were rated as more competent by parents, teachers, and peers
- Earned more money

The ability to *delay gratification* at a young age was strongly linked to long-term life success.

What is the problem?

The decision-making problem identified by the marshmallow experiment involves managing the tension between short-term and long-term gains.

American businesses have long faced criticism for prioritizing immediate results over long-term strategies. Executives often receive compensation based on quarterly and annual performance metrics. However, many initiatives, such as building new factories or pursuing research and development, take years or even decades to yield returns. This tendency also affects younger professionals, who often overvalue short-term results.

"The stock market is a device for transferring money from the impatient to the patient." – *Warren Buffett*

What is the Marshmallow Mental Model?

The Marshmallow Framework recognizes that the solution weighs short-term versus long-term payoffs. It offers a logical step-by-step method to assist you in comparing the choices. However, the final decision is a judgment call that involves values, perception, and individual preferences.

A Real Business Example: Warren Buffett

When Warren Buffett was a young boy growing up in Omaha, he loved soda—especially Coca-Cola. One summer, he realized he could either *spend* his few dollars buying Coke to drink immediately...or he could *buy* six-packs wholesale and *sell* the individual bottles for a profit.

Instead of giving in to the temptation to drink the Coke himself, Buffett set up a small stand and started selling each bottle for more than he paid. He then used the profits to buy more Coke, newspapers, and small investments.

That single act of delaying the *pleasure of drinking* the Coke led him to understand the power of *delayed gratification* and *compounding growth*. Buffett is now one of the wealthiest investors in history. He still loves Coca-Cola and in fact, his company Berkshire Hathaway is a major shareholder in the soft drink company.

"Drink the Coke now, and it's gone. Sell the Coke, reinvest, and someday you might own the whole bottling plant." – *Warren Buffett*

Key Takeaways

If you can't delay gratification, you're more likely to:

- Abandon long-term goals for short-term comfort.
- Lose the gains from compounding in investing, learning, and relationships.
- Make decisions based on feelings rather than strategic outcomes.

If you can delay gratification, you're more likely to:

- Build resilience and future vision.

- Achieve greater success over time through compounded efforts.
- Make decisions based on future-oriented reasoning.

How to Apply the Marshmallow Mental Model

Step 1: The first step, while obvious, can be difficult. You need to clarify your true objective.

Ask yourself:

"Is my primary goal short-term gain (e.g., cash flow, quick wins)?"

"Or is it long-term growth (e.g., brand equity, market share, personal wealth)?"

Your action:

Write a one-sentence strategic goal. For example: "I want to build a $10M brand in five years, not just earn $250K this year."

Step 2: Map out your projected immediate vs. future outcomes. Create a simple matrix. This example is from a real business.

Immediate Action	Sell company now
Immediate Reward	Quick $750K payout
Delayed Action	Grow for 5 more years
Future Reward	Potential $10M valuation

Your action:

Physically map your options. Seeing them visually forces rational comparison instead of emotional reactions.

Step 3: Assess the certainty and risk of your projections. Ask:

- "How sure is the delayed reward? What is the numerical probability?"
- "What risks threaten this estimation?"
- "What safeguards can I build to reduce risk while waiting?"

Your action:

Assign probability estimates to outcomes (even imperfect ones).

For example: "Eighty percent chance of reaching $10M valuation if I hit key milestones."

Step 4: It can be hard to delay gratification. It's helpful to do two things:

- Long-term delays can feel unbearable without small victories. Create staged goals and milestone rewards. For example, set interim markers (monthly, quarterly) with celebrations or bonuses. "If we hit $1.5M ARR this year, founders take a $100K bonus."
- Commit to a time-boxed review. Set a checkpoint date where you will reassess your decision based on real data, not emotions.

These steps are designed to help you make a rational business decision. Behavioral economics shows that our decisions are also influenced by emotions, ego, and personal preferences.

To that end, I suggest two additional steps:

- Visualize your choices. Imagine what taking the short-term option will feel like. How happy or satisfied will you be now and later? Do the same with the long-term choice. Which option appeals to you more? Does one feel more comfortable than the other? You may share your thoughts with your partner, close friend, or colleague.

Expressing your thoughts and feelings can bring clarity.
- Look at your opportunity costs. Make a "future loss" list, not just a "future gain" list.

Example: "Selling early = no legacy brand, no industry dominance, no multiplier on future ventures."

Related Frameworks

- Can you have your marshmallow and eat it too? If you can find a way to make your decision reversible by using **Bezos's Two-Way Doors** you might be able to do just that.
- **Inversion** or thinking backward from the desired outcome is one way of assessing whether you should wait for better outcomes in the future.
- **Tame and Wicked Problems** – wicked or complex problems where variables affect each other are the most difficult to calculate present vs. future values.

"Compounding only works if you can give it time. Time is the most important force behind success." – *Morgan Housel, The Psychology of Money*

Chapter 10
Dr. Phil

Whether or not you enjoy watching television's *Dr. Phil Show*, the two standard questions he often asks guests merits our attention. They are:

"What were you thinking?" and "How did that work out for you?"

What is the problem?

We are all susceptible to impulsive decisions. These can stem from biased thinking, advertising, peer influence, groupthink, or even the desire to avoid responsibility. Impulsivity can be damaging to personal relationships, which is why Dr. Phil poses these two questions. It also adversely affects business and professional careers.

"Until you make the unconscious conscious, it will direct your life, and you will call it fate." – *Carl Jung*

What is the Dr. Phil Mental Model?

Psychologists refer to this concept as "reflective accountability." Reflective accountability involves taking responsibility not only for your actions but also for the thought processes behind those actions, while continuously assessing how your decisions, assumptions, and impacts correspond with your values and goals.

Asking yourself Dr. Phil's simple questions will help you analyze your assumptions, thought processes, and the potential outcomes of your decisions. This provides three benefits:

1. Ownership of your decisions: You are less prone to blaming circumstances or others for your decisions. You own them, including the thought processes that led to them.
2. Alignment with your goals: You check whether your daily actions and decisions adhere to your larger mission, standards, and vision.
3. Continuous learning through honest reflection: Mistakes aren't just things to fix. They are sources of insight to improve future decision-making.

A Real Business Example: Blockbuster's Failure to Adapt

In the early 2000s, Blockbuster was the king of the movie rental business, with thousands of stores worldwide and significant profits from late fees. However, with the emergence of Netflix—initially a DVD mailing service that later transitioned to streaming—Blockbuster's reign came to an end. As of this book's printing, only one Blockbuster store remains in Alaska. "What were they thinking?" The executives at Blockbuster dismissed Netflix as a niche business, believing that people preferred visiting physical stores and viewed late fees as a lucrative source of revenue. They even had the opportunity to buy Netflix for $50 million in 2000 but declined the offer, choosing instead to focus on preserving their traditional business model.

"How did that work out for them?" As streaming became the preferred method of consuming media, Blockbuster's reluctance to adapt resulted in its downfall. The company declared bankruptcy in 2010, while Netflix evolved into a multi-billion-dollar entertainment giant.

Key Takeaways

- Challenge your assumptions: Regularly reevaluate your motives, the reasons behind your decisions, and whether they align with reality.
- Honestly evaluate outcomes: Be brutally honest when assessing results. Conducting debriefs where you objectively analyze results can uncover blind spots or flawed thinking patterns.

Learn from your mistakes: Failures provide valuable lessons, but only if you critically analyze and reflect on what went wrong.

How to Apply the Dr. Phil Framework

The Dr. Phil Framework poses questions to encourage individuals to reflect on their past actions. You can also envision yourself in the future as if you are looking back at your current choices.

For example, if you are considering creating a supporting YouTube channel for your enterprise, you would ask yourself Dr. Phil's questions. It would be something like this:

"What am I thinking?"

- Doing videos could be fun.
- Videos may help sales of my product or service.
- Seeing myself on YouTube would boost my ego.

"How will this work out for me?"

- Creating videos every week is work, but it could also be rewarding.
- Social media is another way to market my offerings.
- I don't care about social media, as evidenced by the fact that I don't use it much now.

Asking yourself these kinds of questions forces you to clarify your motives, including your ego. It also makes you question assumptions that this is a productive way to market your offerings.

Asking yourself these questions will help you be more aware of your beliefs, intentions, and reasoning.

Related Frameworks

- **Inversion** or thinking backward from the desired outcome is another way of avoiding failure due to poor thinking. Immediate gratification or focusing on short-term goals can cause you to make rash decision that you later regret.
- Use the **Marshmallows** mental model to avoid this error.
- The **No-cost Consultant** is an easy way to check your thinking.

"Insanity is doing the same thing over and over again and expecting different results." – *often attributed to Albert Einstein*

Part III Principles of Clarity

Chapter 11
First Principles Thinking

Remember when your Amazon orders were delivered by FedEx and UPS? What caused that change? Jeff Bezos aimed to reduce Amazon's delivery costs. Everyone assumed that utilizing the existing delivery systems was essential, negotiating lower prices based on volume. Instead, Bezos analyzed the problem down to its core components: transporting his company's parcels swiftly and affordably to delivery trucks, and then efficiently organizing the truck routes. He didn't take for granted that the current delivery networks executed either task effectively. By establishing Amazon's own fulfillment centers and delivery network, Bezos cut costs, gained total control over the supply chain, and transformed e-commerce.

What is the problem?

When solving problems, we often make two types of errors:

1. Using flawed assumptions
2. Thinking too quickly

Both are bad practices, and when you're trying to be innovative, they can really hold you back. These errors can lead you to think incrementally when more groundbreaking ideas are possible.

What is the First Principles Mental Model?

First Principles thinking is a problem-solving method that breaks down complex problems into their most basic elements and builds solutions from the ground up. Instead of using analogies or relying on what others have done, this approach challenges assumptions, identifies core truths, and generates new insights.

If your company struggles with retaining customers, instead of copying competitors' loyalty programs, break the problem into three **First Principles** questions:

- Why do customers leave? (Facts and not assumptions)
- What do customers fundamentally value? (Again, facts and not assumptions)
- How can I address the reasons customers leave by giving them the value they want?

By examining the problem from this more basic perspective, you may uncover valuable insights, such as improving communication or streamlining your product, rather than focusing solely on perks or discounts.

A Real Business Example: SpaceX and Rocket Costs

When Elon Musk founded SpaceX, launching rockets into space was prohibitively expensive, costing hundreds of millions of dollars. Industry experts believed this was an unavoidable cost.

Using the **First Principles** approach, Musk asked:

1. What are the essential components of a rocket?
2. What are the raw materials (e.g., aluminum, titanium, composites, fuel) needed to build a rocket, and how much do they cost?

By breaking down the problem into its fundamental components, Musk discovered that traditional manufacturers were charging significantly more for materials than their actual costs. This insight enabled SpaceX to design reusable rockets from the ground up, dramatically decreasing launch costs and disrupting the aerospace industry.

"You have to find a way to achieve the same result without breaking the laws of physics by taking a fresh approach." – *Elon Musk*

Key Takeaways

The steps of the **First Principles** framework are:

- Deconstruct problems: Identify assumptions and separate them from the fundamental truths of a situation.
- Focus on fundamentals: Ask, "What do we know for sure?" and use these facts to develop solutions.
- Challenge conventional wisdom: Avoid blindly following precedents or industry norms; seek unique perspectives.
- Encourage innovation: By starting from scratch, First Principles thinking fosters creativity and non-traditional solutions.

First Principles thinking helps you to question assumptions, think critically, and discover groundbreaking solutions. Whether you are launching rockets, managing a business, or addressing everyday problems, this framework offers a roadmap for innovative and cost-effective solutions.

How to Apply the First Principles Mental Model

1. Define the problem clearly. Start by stating exactly what you're trying to solve or understand.

Example: "Why is this product so expensive to build?"

2. Break it into fundamentals. Strip away assumptions, conventions, and analogies. Ask:

- What do I *know* to be true?
- What elements are essential?
- What factors are just inherited thinking?

Example: Instead of saying "batteries cost $200/kWh," ask "What materials make up a battery? What are their costs?"

3. Analyze each component deeply. Understand how each fundamental part works and why. Research raw facts and challenge conventional wisdom.

4. Reconstruct a new solution. Use your insight to rebuild your understanding or design a new path forward from scratch, free of assumptions.

Related Frameworks

- In Step 3, use the **Six Honest Serving Men** to drill deeper into each component.
- **Divergent and Convergent Thinking** is a tool for systematically checking your assumptions and then drawing conclusions.

"First principles thinking is the act of boiling a process down to the fundamental parts that you know are true and building up from there." – *James Clear*

Chapter 12
Occam's Razor

At the Toyota Motor Hokkaido (TMH) manufacturing plant in Japan, a section of the assembly line kept experiencing unexpected power outages. Engineers were baffled. They brought in electrical specialists, reviewed schematics, and even considered rewiring entire sections of the factory.

Some of the theories floated:

- Is there a voltage drop from the city's electrical grid?
- Has the automated machine developed a software bug?
- Could a faulty sensor be causing a series of cascading failures?

After days of costly downtime, a junior technician who was new to the plant simply walked the length of the affected section looking for anything unusual. He noticed something odd: a cleaning crew's industrial vacuum cord was plugged into the same outlet as the critical automated multiprocessor that controlled the machinery. He discovered that every time he turned on the vacuum, it tripped a breaker that automatically reset itself later.

What is the problem?

Occam's Razor addresses the issue of overcomplicated explanations or solutions, particularly when several hypotheses are available.

"Keep it simple stupid." – *Kelly Johnson, lead engineer at the Lockheed Skunk Works*

What is the Occam's Razor Mental Model?

Occam's Razor is a problem-solving principle suggesting that the simplest solution is often the best. More precisely, it recommends that among competing hypotheses, one should select the option with the fewest assumptions. Named after the fourteenth-century philosopher William of Ockham, this model is widely applied in science, logic, and business to eliminate unnecessary complexity.

A Real Business Example: Southwest Airlines' Strategy

In the 1970s, most airlines competed by offering various add-on accoutrements. They offered luxurious in-flight meals, multiple-size planes and cabin classes, and extensive route options. Herb Kelleher, co-founder of Southwest Airlines, applied a simpler model: offer low-cost, point-to-point travel with a single aircraft type (Boeing 737) and no frills. Southwest was more like riding a bus. It had open seating on a first-come, first-served basis. By simplifying the business model, Southwest cut maintenance costs, improved scheduling, and turned a profit while competitors struggled.

Southwest Airlines was Occam's Razor at work. Instead of assuming that passengers needed luxury, multiple classes, or international routes, Kelleher assumed they simply wanted to get from Point A to Point B cheaply and reliably. That simpler hypothesis—and operating model—won.

Key Takeaways

- Simplest is not always correct, but it's usually the best starting point: Occam's Razor doesn't guarantee that the simple solution is right, but that it's the best place to begin.
- Simplicity drives clarity. Reducing unnecessary features or processes can make operations more efficient and understandable.
- Avoid overfitting your strategy. More complex assumptions or hypotheses often introduce fragility and hidden risks.
- Useful in meetings and product design. When a team proposes multiple explanations or features, ask, "What's the simplest explanation or version that still solves the problem?"

How to Apply the Occam's Razor Mental Model

1. Clearly define the problem in its simplest terms. Think "How would I describe this to an eighth grader?" Do this before trying to speculate on possible causes or solutions. We suggest actually writing it down to ensure you keep it simple.

For example: "Why are customer cancellations up twenty-five percent this month?"

2. List all of the plausible explanations that come to mind. Just list them. Don't go down the rabbit hole of discussing them in detail. Brainstorm every reasonable explanation or course of action. Don't worry yet about which is better.

Continuing our example:

- Our website is down intermittently
- A competitor launched a promotion
- Customer service wait times have increased
- A recent policy change may have confused customers

3. Eliminate the choices that have extra assumptions or beliefs. Now use Occam's Razor to strip out solutions that require multiple assumptions or complex chains of cause and effect. Look for the more straightforward explanations grounded in direct evidence.

For example:

> Eliminate this: "There's a new shadow competitor with an identical product who's poaching our customers using a secret AI algorithm."
>
> Keep this: "The new cancellation policy has unclear language."

4. Test the simplest explanation first. Implement a low-cost or low-risk test based on the simplest explanation. See if addressing that resolves the issue.

For example: "Review the cancellation pages for long sentences, corporate speak, or unclear language. Revise and monitor cancellation rates for seven days."

Escalate only if necessary. If the simplest solution doesn't resolve the issue, then escalate to more complex scenarios or solutions. This is also a good opportunity to use the **No-cost Consultant** mental model, as individuals unfamiliar with the problem may perceive the situation more clearly.

Related Frameworks

- Utilizing the **No-cost Consultant** mental model might assist you in applying Occam's Razor. Often, those unfamiliar with a problem perceive it in its simplest form.
- **Attribution Error** can prevent you from recognizing simplicity as you attribute events to the character of others instead of the facts.
- Using the **Pareto Principle (80/20 Rule)** can help you focus on the 20% of actions that deliver 80% of the results.

"Why did the chicken cross the road? To get to the other side." – *children's joke*

Chapter 13
Inversion

SAVE WOMEN IN CHILDBIRTH

How am I contributing to their deaths?

In the 1800s, hospitals had alarmingly high rates of maternal mortality due to *puerperal fever*, also known as childbed fever. Doctors and medical students were puzzled as they searched for ways to improve patient survival. They asked, "What can we do to save these women?" In Vienna, Austria, Dr. Ignaz Semmelweis flipped the question around and asked, "What are we doing that may contribute to their deaths?"

This shift in perspective prompted a deeper understanding of potentially harmful behaviors or practices. Semmelweis observed that doctors at Vienna General Hospital often performed autopsies before delivering babies without washing their hands. He theorized that invisible "particles" from dead bodies were being transmitted to patients during childbirth, causing infections.

To test his theory, Semmelweis implemented a strict policy at the hospital requiring all medical staff to wash their hands with a chlorinated lime solution before handling patients. The results were astounding: maternal mortality rates plummeted from eighteen percent to less than two percent. Semmelweis became known as the "savior of mothers." Unfortunately, his findings were not widely accepted until years after his death, when Louis Pasteur confirmed the germ theory.

Through this process of reverse thinking—focusing on what to avoid rather than what to add—Semmelweis discovered a simple yet life-saving practice that is now a fundamental component of modern medicine. Google honored his "backward thinking."

What is the problem?

In our efforts to succeed, we often overlook the potential causes of failure. If we focus solely on success and don't strive to avoid failure, we tend to take incremental steps and cling to our cognitive biases. We need a way to make our thinking more objective and empirical.

What is the Inversion Mental Model?

Inversion is a problem-solving technique where you think about the opposite of what you want to achieve. Instead of asking, "How do I succeed?" you ask, "What would cause me to fail?" You gain insights that help you achieve your goal by identifying what to avoid. By exploring potential obstacles and pitfalls, you gain insight into actions or strategies to avoid while identifying potential paths toward success. Investor and billionaire Charlie Munger popularized this concept with his mantra, "Invert, always invert!"

A Real Business Example: Tesla's Approach to Overcoming EV Doubt

Tesla applied the **Inversion** mental model when tackling the challenges of selling electric vehicles (EVs) in a market dominated by internal combustion engine cars. Instead of asking

"How can we convince people to buy EVs?", Tesla asked, "Why might people be hesitant to purchase EVs?"

Obstacles to overcome:

Personal perception. EV owners and Prius drivers in particular were perceived as overly proud and condescending toward those who didn't drive hybrids. This perception was famously satirized in a 2006 episode of *South Park*, titled **"Smug Alert!"** that mocked EV owners.

Range anxiety. People feared running out of battery while driving. The lack of available charging infrastructure reinforced this concern.

Lack of appeal. Perception that EVs are inferior or unappealing compared to traditional vehicles.

To tackle the inverted questions, Tesla invested in the development of high-performance battery systems and established a global Supercharger network to alleviate concerns regarding range and charging capabilities.

It positioned its cars as luxury, high-performance vehicles, effectively debunking the notion that EVs were undesirable or less powerful than traditional cars. "Driving a Tesla is sexy. It's like piloting a spaceship; smooth, fast, and exhilarating."

By focusing on and resolving potential barriers that could impede success, Tesla was able to shift public perception of EVs and establish itself as a leader in the industry.

Key Takeaways

- Avoid problems. Inverting the question of how to achieve your goals will help you identify potential pitfalls and preventive measures.
- Simplification. Inverting simplifies complex problems: By flipping a problem on its head, you may uncover insights

that are not apparent when only focusing on success.

- Prioritize robustness. **Inversion** helps ensure your strategy is resilient by addressing potential threats or vulnerabilities.
- Enhance decision-making. Thinking in opposites challenges assumptions and exposes blind spots, leading to more balanced and informed choices.

How to Apply the Inversion Mental Model

1. Define the goal. Start by clearly defining what you want to achieve. Then flip the goal upside down and ask yourself, "What could completely hinder success or result in failure?" For example, if your goal is to increase customer loyalty, consider asking, "What would cause customers to leave?"

2. Identify actions to avoid. Carefully consider the actions, behaviors, or systems that could lead to the worst-case scenario. This step involves recognizing potential risks or pitfalls, such as poor customer service, unreliable products, or unclear pricing, to prevent losing customers.

3. Create a list of contraries. Once you have identified what to avoid, consider how to eliminate or mitigate those risks. For example, if unreliable products are a concern, invest in quality control systems and implement a customer feedback loop to ensure high product standards.

4. Use your inverted question to challenge assumptions. **Inversion** helps reveal blind spots by prompting you to consider scenarios you might otherwise overlook. Challenge your existing plans by asking: "What if we're mistaken?" "What unintended consequences could arise?" For example, if you're launching a new product, ask yourself, "What if the market rejects it?" Use this insight to refine your product offering and marketing.

5. Test preventive measures. Implement solutions or strategies based on your inverted analysis to avoid potential failure points. Regularly revisit and refine these measures. For example, if you're concerned about poor customer service, provide thorough training for employees and establish a system to monitor customer satisfaction.

Related Frameworks

- **First Principles Thinking** is the process of breaking problems down into fundamental truths and reasoning from there instead of relying on assumptions.
- It is the opposite of **Inversion** but serves a similar purpose.
- It can help you check your **Inversion Thinking**.

"Eliminating foolishness is easier than seeking brilliance." – *Charlie Munger*

Chapter 14
Six Honest Serving Men

In 2009, Airbnb was struggling. They had launched, but almost no one was booking rooms. Founders Brian Chesky and Joe Gebbia sat down to ask themselves the Six Honest Serving Men questions:

- *What* is stopping people from booking?
- *Why* are listings getting clicks but not bookings?
- *When* do people abandon the site?
- *How* can we make listings more appealing?
- *Where* are the worst-performing cities?
- *Who* is our real customer: the host or the guest?

By posing these questions, they identified the root causes of the issue. Among the revelations, one in particular surprised them: the photos in most listings were unappealing. They were often blurry, dark, and generally unprofessional in appearance.

The photos made the listings appear questionable. So Chesky

and Gebbia rented a good camera, visited New York hosts, and took better photos. Bookings doubled within two months. By accurately identifying the major causes of the problem, they saved the company.

What is the problem?

Humans are naturally inclined to jump to conclusions, act on assumptions, and see only part of the picture. This can lead to:

- Shallow thinking
- Missed risks and opportunities
- Misunderstood problems
- Poor decision-making

"We get trapped by what we think we know instead of fully exploring what we need to know." – *Unknown*

What is the Six Honest Serving Men Mental Model?

Kipling's poem serves as a mnemonic or memory aid to help recall the six questions you should ask to properly define a situation or problem.

"I keep six honest serving-men (They taught me all I knew); Their names are What and Why and When And How and Where and Who." — *Rudyard Kipling*, from *The Elephant's Child*

This is sometimes referred to as the Five Ws and an H.

In *Thinking, Fast and Slow*, Daniel Kahneman describes how our brain defaults to fast, intuitive "System 1" thinking, which is efficient but prone to error. By asking the right questions to define a situation, you slow your brain into System 2 thinking: deliberate, analytical, and more accurate. When you slow down, you force yourself to see more possibilities instead of seizing the first answer that feels right.

Good problem-solving often follows four steps in sequence:

1. Define the problem
2. Explore options
3. Evaluate
4. Decide

The six types of questions are most often used in the first step, but they can also be used in the other steps.

A Real Business Example: Toyota Engineering

Toyota famously uses the Five Whys technique, repeatedly asking "Why?" to find the root cause of engineering problems. It's part of "The Toyota Way." However, at the leadership level, when they restructured supply chains after the 2011 tsunami, they broadened the inquiry using the Six Honest Serving Men Framework to answer *What* caused the disruption.

- *Why* were we unprepared for a multi-site failure?
- *When* did warning signs first appear?
- *How* can we build more resilient supply chains?
- *Where* are our vulnerabilities geographically concentrated?
- *Who* is responsible for contingency planning?

By systematically addressing all six question types—not just "why"—Toyota future-proofed its supply systems against future shocks. They moved from reactive problem-solving to proactive strategy building.

Key Takeaways

- Asking the six types of questions outlined in the poem will help you define problems or situations. This also slows your thinking to System 2 thinking, which is more intentional and thorough.
- Asking from multiple angles invites diverse perspectives, preventing narrow-mindedness. You can apply this

model in any situation: problem-solving, strategy, or planning.

How to Apply the Six Honest Serving Men Mental Model

When applying the **Six Honest Serving Men** framework, don't use the questions superficially. Dig deeper until you achieve the purpose of that question.

1. Start with "What" to define the core problem

- Ask: What exactly is happening?
- Purpose: Clarifies the real issue versus symptoms or coincidental events.

Example: *What is causing our customers to stop renewing subscriptions?*

2. Then ask "Why" to understand the root causes

- Ask: Why is this happening? (and keep asking "why" multiple times—as in the Toyota "Five Whys" technique).
- Purpose: This digs beneath surface explanations to the source of the issue.

Example: *Why are customers leaving?* Answer: Because onboarding is confusing.

3. Next, ask, "Who" to identify the people involved

- Ask: Who is involved in this? Who is affected, and even who could help?
- Purpose: Maps out who must be considered or involved in solving it.

Example: *Who interacts with new customers? Who can fix the onboarding flow?*

4. Follow with "Where" to pinpoint context

- Ask: Where is the problem happening?
- Purpose: Locates the environments, departments, or touchpoints involved.

Example: *Where are customers dropping off?* Answer: On the welcome page after signing up.

5. Ask "When" to understand timing and patterns

- Ask: When does the problem occur? Is there a pattern or sequence?
- Purpose: Spots trends, cycles, or triggering events.

Example: *When do most cancellations happen?* Answer: Within the first three days.

6. Finally, ask "How" to explore causal factors or start on solutions

- Ask: How can this be happening? How can we prevent it?
- Purpose: Moves from diagnosis to solution design, deliberately.

Example: *How can we make onboarding simpler and more engaging?*

This sequence is recommended, but the process is iterative. When you ask "When," you may discover something that brings you back to "Why?"

Related Frameworks

- The **Tame and Wicked Problems** mental model will help you identify the complexity level of the problem.
- You can use the **Six Honest Serving Men** in both phases of **Divergent and Convergent Thinking.**

"If I had an hour to solve a problem, I'd spend fifty-five minutes thinking about the problem and five minutes thinking about solutions." – *Albert Einstein*

Chapter 15
No-cost Consultant

During the winter months, Lisa, the owner of Two Rosters Ice Cream Shop in Raleigh, North Carolina, faced a decline in sales. She came up with a unique idea: asking her young customers for suggestions.

Lisa created a "Kids' Club" suggestion box and offered a free small scoop of ice cream to any child who submitted an idea. To her surprise, the suggestions from these "no-cost consultants" were valuable and innovative. Ideas such as hot cocoa with mini marshmallows, make your own sundae nights, and a loyalty program for families were among the kids' suggestions.

The results were impressive:

- Hot cocoa became a popular winter treat, attracting families on cold days.
- "Make Your Own Sundae Nights" became a weekly event that brought in crowds and generated buzz.

- The family loyalty program led to repeat visits and increased sales, even during slow months.

What is the problem?

We would like to hire highly qualified consultants to assist us with our problems; however, they are expensive. We need a way to obtain quality advice and fresh ideas without spending a lot of money.

What is the No-cost Consultant Mental Model?

The No-Cost Consultant framework suggests that you can obtain valuable information and advice from free sources. While we typically consider free sources to be things like Google searches, publications, and reference materials, this mental model focuses instead on people.

This approach relies on active listening, thoughtful questioning, and utilizing real-world input to enrich ideas and solutions.

A Real Business Example: Sara Blakely of Spanx

Sara Blakely had the idea of footless pantyhose, but she lacked the money or experience to start a business. Knowing her idea was unique, she cold-called the Georgia State Bar Association and asked for help finding a female patent attorney as she thought another woman would "get it." She received a referral—an attorney who not only advised her on how to file her first patent but also provided her a discount. That patent protected Blakely's product and helped Spanx grow into a billion-dollar business. The free help from Georgia's State Bar Association showcases the tangible value of a "no-cost consultant" approach that kicked off her endeavor, compared to traditional paid arrangements or market research methods.

Key Takeaways

- "Talk is cheap." Take advantage of it.
- Valuable perspectives come from various sources: Customers, employees, and stakeholders can all provide valuable input that can lead to problem-solving or opportunities for growth.
- Nurture involvement and trust: Seeking input from others not only promotes loyalty but also shows that a business values its community.
- Innovate affordably: Crowd-sourcing ideas is a cost-effective method of innovation compared to traditional consulting or research.

How to Apply the No-cost Consultant Mental Model

- If you ask someone for advice, you may feel some obligation to follow it. However, if you ask, "May I borrow your perception?" and then describe your situation, there isn't that sense of indebtedness.
- Once you've asked someone for their perception, ask them who else you should talk to. You may be surprised at the level of expertise you'll access for free.
- One of the biggest hurdles in using the **No-cost Consulting** framework is the fear that someone will steal your ideas. In reality, most ideas are not particularly unique, and people are generally too busy with their own priorities to pursue someone else's concept.
- If your idea really is unique, it's relatively easy and cheap to get trademarks and patents.

Related Frameworks

- The **Six Honest Serving Men** mental model can be used to guide the conversation when consulting with someone unfamiliar with your problem.

"He who asks is a fool for five minutes, but he who does not ask remains a fool forever." – *Chinese Proverb*

Part IV: Decision Analysis Tools

Chapter 16
Divergent and Convergent Thinking

"Tesco's CEO resigns for using the wrong decision-making process." In 2007, Tesco—the largest grocery retailer in the UK—tried to break into the US market with a new brand called Fresh & Easy. The concept was based on the success of Tesco's stores back home, focusing on ready-to-eat meals and a simplified shopping experience. But the venture soon hit several roadblocks.

- **Cultural misalignment**: American consumers favored stocking up on groceries during weekly trips over the frequent, smaller purchases typical in the UK.
- **Lack of local insight**: Tesco didn't investigate the diverse shopping habits across US regions.
- **Operational challenges**: Significant investments in automation fell flat, as many American shoppers valued high-touch service over Tesco's high-tech approach.

By 2013, after spending over $1 billion, Tesco closed all of its US Fresh & Easy stores.

"I truly gave it my all when I became CEO, but ultimately, I am accountable to our investors. I didn't ask enough questions before deciding to enter the US market." – *Philip Clarke, Tesco CEO*

What is the problem?

When people generate and evaluate ideas simultaneously, they often censor themselves or dismiss novel concepts too quickly. Similarly, if they remain in brainstorm mode for too long, they fail to commit to action.

What is the Divergent and Convergent Thinking Mental Model?

Decision-making naturally involves two parts: generating options and then choosing among them. Leaders can err in either phase. Prolonged divergence can create "paralysis by analysis." Teams may become trapped in an endless cycle of idea generation. Without a clear path forward, decision-making grinds to a halt, leaving innovation purely theoretical and preventing progress.

For example, Yahoo! had the opportunity to acquire Google when it was a start-up. Internal debates and prolonged evaluations took so long that they missed the chance. On the other hand, converging too soon can lead to rushed decisions.

Sometimes, one jumps to conclusions without adequately exploring alternatives. It's easy to latch onto the first idea, which can result in uninspired solutions, missed opportunities, and a tendency toward confirmation bias.

For example, Tesco launched its US product based solely on internal opinions. They did not consider local client preferences, cultural differences, or the operational challenges of a different market.

Think of it as a funnel: Divergence opens up all the possibilities—what could be possible?—while convergence narrows those down to what is optimal.

"You can't create and criticize at the same time." – *Alex Osborn, the inventor of brainstorming*

A Real Business Example: IDEO's Design Thinking Process

IDEO, the globally renowned consulting firm, always incorporates both divergent and convergent thinking into its famous design process.

- **Empathize and ideate (Divergent):** IDEO generates a wide array of solutions to address a customer's pain points. They welcome wild and unconventional ideas.
- **Prototype and test (Convergent):** Selecting and refining the top ideas into actionable, testable prototypes.

In one case, IDEO was hired to improve a hospital's patient experience. IDEO invited input from everyone: janitors, nurses, food service workers, doctors, and, of course, patients.

After gathering hundreds of suggestions, IDEO converged on a new patient journey that featured clearer signage, reduced wait times, and improved bedside communication.

Key Takeaways

- Use divergent thinking to unlock creativity and avoid premature conclusions.
- Use convergent thinking to evaluate ideas methodically and act decisively.
- Switching consciously between these two modes is a hallmark of effective strategic thinking.

How to Apply the Divergent and Convergent Thinking Mental Model

Step 1: First diverge. Explore options widely.

Goal: Generate as many ideas, perspectives, or possibilities as possible *without judging them.*

Ask yourself:

- What are all the ways to solve this problem?
- What approaches have never been tried before?
- How might a competitor address this?
- What would a child suggest?
- What would we do if budget were not an issue?

Some useful tools include:

- Brainstorming sessions
- "How might we?" questions
- Reverse thinking (for example, "How could we make this worse?")

Step 2: Converge thoughtfully. Evaluate and decide.

Goal: Narrow down the possibilities to select the most feasible, effective, or mission-aligned path.

Consider:

- Which idea best aligns with our mission and goals?
- What is the risk versus return for each option?
- What do the data and evidence suggest?
- What is the first small test we could run?

Useful tools include:

- Dotmocracy or multi-voting
- Decision matrices
- First-principles filtering

The key is to diverge to uncover possibilities and converge to clarify and decide. These steps should be distinct rather than merged into a single decision-making moment.

Related Frameworks

- The **First Principles Thinking** model can be used in combination with **Divergent and Convergent Thinking.** You can break problems down into fundamental truths and then use this model on the pieces.
- The **No-cost Consultant** model is a way to check your thinking during both steps of this model.
- The more complex the problem, the more divergent thinking you must do. **Tame and Wicked Problems** model can be used to diagnose the nature of the problem.

"The key to good decision-making is not knowledge. It is understanding how to use knowledge. Divergent and convergent thinking must be sequenced, not blurred." – *Roger Martin, former Dean of the Rotman School of Management*

Chapter 17
Pareto Principle

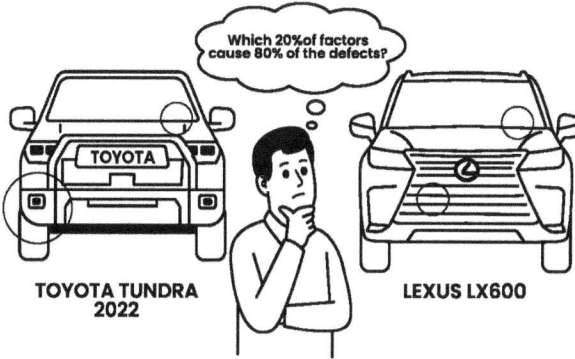

The Toyota brand is known for its reliability. However, in 2022, dealers reported that Toyota's Tundra pickups and Lexus LX600 luxury SUVs were stalling for no apparent reason. Inspections revealed that debris from the manufacturing process might not have been cleared from the engine, potentially leading to engine knocking, rough running, or stalling, which increases the risk of a crash. Internal quality audits indicated that eighty percent of vehicle defects originated from just twenty percent of the manufacturing steps or suppliers.

Rather than scrutinizing every process equally, Toyota engineers focused intensely on the few chokepoints causing most of the issues. Eventually, they discovered that these twenty percent had installed new robotic arms as part of the upgrade process.

What is the problem?

In business and life, we often treat all tasks, customers, and efforts as equally valuable, which leads to wasted time, energy, and capital. It's easy to become overwhelmed by trying to do everything instead of focusing on what is most important. We can easily squander time on low-value activities, resulting in decision fatigue and ineffective problem-solving.

"The key to success is not doing more, but doing more of what matters most." – *Greg McKeown*, author of *Essentialism*

What is the Pareto Principle Mental Model?

The **Pareto Principle**, also known as the **80/20 Rule**, is a mental model that states that roughly 80% of outcomes result from 20% of causes. This principle suggests that a small number of inputs (the "vital few") are often responsible for the majority of results, while most inputs (the "trivial many") have a much smaller impact.

The principle was named after the Italian economist Vilfredo Pareto, who observed in the late nineteenth century that 80% of Italy's land was owned by 20% of the population. His further studies revealed that 20% of the olive trees produced 80% of the crop. This concept has since been broadly applied in business, economics, time management, and decision-making.

Example applications:

- Business: 80% of sales come from 20% of customers.
- Time management: 20% of tasks yield 80% of productivity.
- Quality control: 20% of defects cause 80% of problems.

A Real Business Example: US Healthcare Costs

A study by the Kaiser Family Foundation (KFF) found that "a minority of patients (20%) consume the majority of resources (80%) due to chronic illnesses, end-of-life care, or multiple hospitalizations. Meanwhile, the remaining 80% of patients contribute far less to overall spending."

This led to a KFF policy design proposal focus that "case management and preventive care should be targeted at the top 20% to lower system-wide expenses."

Key Takeaways

A small portion of inputs drive most results

- Roughly 20% of causes lead to 80% of effects.
- Identify the "vital few" vs. the "trivial many."

Not everything deserves your equal attention

- Time, money, and energy are limited. Use them where returns are disproportionately high.
- Avoid the trap of treating all tasks as equally important.

This is a guideline, not a law

- It doesn't have to be 80/20 exactly. It may be 70/30, 90/10, etc.
- The core idea is imbalance: inputs and outputs are rarely distributed evenly.

How to Apply the Pareto Principle Mental Model

Not all efforts are created equal. Concentrate on the 20% of tasks, clients, or skills that yield 80% of your results. Quit glorifying busyness and prioritize effectiveness over mere effort.

Time acts as a leverage tool. Monitor your daily activities to pinpoint what leads to meaningful progress or recognition. Employ methods like time audits or weekly reviews to eliminate low-value tasks.

Master essential skills. You don't have to excel at everything. Focus on a few high-impact skills—such as communication, critical thinking, or sales—that significantly influence your career advancement.

Establish boundaries to prevent burnout. Allocating energy to low-impact tasks (the trivial 80%) results in fatigue without achieving any real progress. Learn to say "no" more often and safeguard your deep work sessions.

Network strategically. A select few of your connections will present the most significant career opportunities. Focus on nurturing these essential relationships instead of trying to network broadly with everyone.

Related Frameworks

- **Tame and Wicked Problems** is another way to categorize problems to facilitate finding solutions. Tame and wicked refer to complicated vs. complex problems.
- When using the **Pareto Principle**, your breakdown of the problem into its components may be influenced by **Confirmation Bias**. Be mindful of the tendency to seek information that supports existing beliefs and counter it.
- The **Eisenhower Matrix** is another way of prioritizing problems based on urgency and importance to focus on what truly matters.

"Eighty percent of consequences come from twenty percent of the causes." – *Vilfredo Pareto (paraphrased from his original economic observations)*

Chapter 18
Expected Value

"How do you win in a game where the deck is stacked against you?"

That was the question haunting Billy Beane, the cash-strapped Oakland A's general manager. While Major League Baseball's richest teams were handing out blank checks for superstar talent, Beane had a different idea: What if he used a different mental model instead of the traditional scouting and baseball statistics models? Armed with spreadsheets, overlooked stats, and a radical mental model called **Expected Value**, he rewrote the rules of baseball.

Instead of trying to outspend the competition, he used the **Expected Value** framework to outsmart his opponents. Beane's team evaluated players not by traditional stats such as batting average, but by on-base percentage (OBP) and slugging percentage, which had higher correlations with actual wins, but were undervalued by the market. A player with an unusual swing or low batting average might still generate more runs per dollar than a star, say by getting walks, *if their OBP was high.*

Beane took repeated low-cost bets on such players. The upside (wins per dollar) far outweighed the downside (a few flops). Over a 162-game season, the *average* performance of these "misfit" players added up to success.

The result? In 2002 the A's won twenty games in a row (an MLB American League record) and made the playoffs that season with one of the lowest payrolls in baseball. Beane didn't try to win each individual bet. He built a portfolio of undervalued players whose combined **Expected Value** translated into wins over time.

"The idea that you can predict what a player is going to do based on his statistics is exactly what we're doing. That's how we make our decisions. We're trying to find value where others aren't looking." – *Billy Beane*

The A's finished high in the American League for the next several seasons until the rest of the teams began to share his approach.

What is the problem?

Humans naturally struggle with uncertainty, especially when outcomes involve probabilities and trade-offs. We often:

- Overweight rare events (e.g., lottery wins)
- Underweight common risks (e.g., car accidents)
- Get swayed by emotion or recent experiences (availability bias, loss aversion)

This leads to poor decisions, like passing up a good investment, launching the wrong product, or wasting time on low-impact activities.

What is the Expected Value Mental Model?

Expected Value (EV) is a fundamental decision-making model from probability theory. It represents the average outcome of a decision if it were repeated many times. It's calculated as:

EV = Σ (Probability of outcome × Value of outcome)

Rather than asking "What could happen?" it asks, "What's the average result if I make this bet over and over?" Here is a simple example.

Let's say you own a coffee shop. One morning, a rich customer offers you a deal:

"Flip a coin. If it's heads, I'll invest $100 in your shop to help you grow. If it's tails, you owe me a free cup of coffee every day for a week (totaling about $35). And I'll make this bet with you every Monday. Deal?"

So, let's run the numbers:

- 50% chance of gaining $100
- 50% chance of losing $35

Your expected value is = (0.5 × $100) + (0.5 × -$35) = $15

That's a nice average gain for a small risk.

He flips the coin. It's tails. You lose…this time.

But the next week, here he comes again. You take the bet again. Third time's the charm. Heads. The customer may be rich, but you're the one making money over time. This is the exact strategy casinos use. It's not about the individual odds, but the average odds.

A Real Business Example: Amazon's Acquisition of Zappos

In 2009, Amazon acquired Zappos for approximately $1.2 billion. At the time, Zappos was profitable but not yet massive. Amazon didn't expect guaranteed outsized returns.

Instead, they likely viewed the acquisition through an Expected Value lens:

- Probability of modest success (70%) × Moderate value gain ($1B)
- Probability of breakout success (20%) × High value gain ($5B)
- Probability of failure (10%) × Loss ($1.2B)

Even if the odds of massive success were low, the potential upside was enough to make the *expected value positive*, justifying the risky investment.

Over time, Zappos became a major contributor to Amazon's customer loyalty playbook—especially in service culture and brand trust—delivering strategic returns well beyond direct financials.

Key Takeaways

- **Expected Value** (EV) enables rational risk-taking.
- It avoids loss aversion bias: People often avoid small losses, even if the expected value is positive.
- Not all high-probability bets are wise: A 90% chance to earn $1 is worse than a 10% chance to earn $100.
- EV depends on both math and judgment: Estimating probabilities and outcomes realistically is critical.

How to Apply the Expected Value Mental Model

Here is a step-by-step guide to applying **Expected Value**:

1. List the Possible Outcomes: Break down what could happen. Be specific.

Example: You're deciding whether to launch a new product.

- Outcome A: It becomes a hit
- Outcome B: It breaks even
- Outcome C: It flops

2. Estimate the Probability of Each Outcome: Use data, judgment, or historical comparisons to guess how likely each one is.

Example:

- Hit: 20% chance
- Break even: 50% chance
- Flop: 30% chance

3. Assign a Value to Each Outcome: Estimate how much you gain or lose in each case.

Example:

- Hit = +$500,000
- Break even = $0
- Flop = -$100,000

4. Do the Math: Multiply and Add: Multiply the value of each outcome by its probability. Then add them together.

Example:

$$EV = (0.2 \times \$500,000) + (0.5 \times \$0) + (0.3 \times -\$100,000)$$
$$EV = \$100,000 - \$30,000 = +\$70,000$$

This means that *on average*, this is a good decision. Even with risk, it has a positive expected value.

5. Compare EV to Alternatives: Repeat the process for your other options. Choose the one with the highest EV, not necessarily the safest.

6. Play the Long Game: You won't win every time, but if you consistently choose options with positive expected value, you win over time.

Action tip: Use ranges if exact numbers are unclear. EV works even with rough estimates.

Related Frameworks

- Every decision has both an emotional and a rational solution. Understanding **Loss Aversion**, or the emotion that people fear losses more than they value equivalent gains will help you make better decisions.

"All life is a series of calculated risks. Nothing is ever guaranteed, but you can tip the odds in your favor." – *Nicole Kidman*

Chapter 19
Opportunity Costs

OPPORTUNITIES

Carlos Ramirez of Charlotte, North Carolina, had always dreamed of owning a restaurant. When he finally had saved $50,000, he had two options:

- Open a brick-and-mortar taco shop with indoor seating and staff.
- Buy and outfit a used food truck for $25,000, and use the remaining funds for marketing and supplies.

His heart was set on "brick and mortar." He ran the numbers, and estimated that the taco shop would take about six months to open, needing permits, and would barely break even during the first year of operation. However, the food truck could launch in thirty days. A number of local festivals, community events, and other locations would provide a lot of potential customers. Ramirez believed his food truck could establish a reputation and build a fan base. After analyzing the numbers, he decided on the truck.

Six months later, Ramirez's food truck had earned $60,000 in profit and had regular customers whom he would see at different events.

The opportunity costs of choosing the taco shop? Missing out on $60,000, many customers, and momentum.

What is the problem?

In business and life, we encounter limited resources: time, money, attention, and energy. Without considering **Opportunity Costs**, people often concentrate on the visible expenses of their choices while disregarding the worth of what they did not select. Moreover, overlooking the **Opportunity Cost** framework makes us susceptible to the sunk cost fallacy, resulting in inefficient resource allocation.

"The most expensive thing you can do is waste time on the wrong opportunity." – *Jeff Bezos*

What is the Opportunity Cost Mental Model?

Opportunity Cost is the value of the next best alternative you give up when you make a choice. It's not just what you spend in time, money, or resources—it's what you could have gained by choosing differently. It's about making comparisons. This model forces you to ask,"What am I giving up by choosing this path?"

Let's look at hypothetical examples—one about money and one about your time.

Money. Imagine you have $100,000 to invest.

- Option A: Invest in launching a new product. Expected return: $20,000
- Option B: Put the money into an index fund. Expected return: $8,000

The Option A Opportunity Cost = $8,000 (Option B) – $20,000 (Option A) = –$12,000 No cost. You made the better choice.

But if you had chosen Option B, the Opportunity Cost = $20,000 (Option A) – $8,000 (Option B) = $12,000. You would have missed out on $12,000 in potential gains.

Time. Imagine you have three hours.

You spend three hours writing social media posts instead of preparing for a sales pitch.

The value of social posts: $100
Potential value of winning the pitch: $5,000
Your opportunity cost is $5,000 – $100 = $4,900

A Real Business Example: Borders Books vs. Amazon vs. Starbucks

This is a fascinating three-way **Opportunity Cost** puzzle. In the early 2000s, Borders Books, once a dominant bookseller, faced a choice: Should it build its own e-commerce infrastructure or outsource its online sales to Amazon?

Borders chose to partner with Amazon rather than invest in its own platform. Borders saw short-term savings and convenience.

The Opportunity Costs were:

- Borders lost the direct relationships with customers (what's that worth?)
- They handed valuable data to a competitor (How do you price that?)
- They missed learning how to build and scale digital channels

But that's not all! Around the same time, Starbucks offered Borders the opportunity to install Starbucks cafés in its stores. Borders declined. Starbucks later surged as a high-traffic consumer cultural hub and brand magnet.

The cost of saying "No": Borders saved on short-term investments but lost future relevance both digitally and experientially.

By 2011:

- Borders filed for bankruptcy.
- Amazon dominated online book sales.
- Starbucks became a retail experience leader.

Key Takeaways

- Every choice carries a hidden cost: It's not just what you spend—it's what you miss.
- **Opportunity Cost** sharpens decision-making, especially under limited resources (time, capital, attention).
- Great companies think in terms of trade-offs. They don't ask, "Can we?" but instead ask, "What's the best use of our resources?"
- Ignoring **Opportunity Costs** can trap you in yesterday's logic (e.g., Blockbuster, Kodak, or Borders).

How to Apply the Opportunity Cost Mental Model

A step-by-step process of calculating **Opportunity Cost**:

1. Define your options

Lay out the two or three most realistic choices you're considering.
"What are my real alternatives here?"

2. Identify the next best alternative

Don't compare against *everything*. Consider only the subsequent best use of your resources (money, time, attention, relationships).

Example: Use how Carlos Ramirez viewed his food truck vs. the strip mall store.

3. Estimate the value of each choice

Ask:
- What's the expected outcome (ROI, learning, reputation, joy)?
- What's the risk or uncertainty?
- What's the time horizon for payoff?
- Try to quantify where possible, but even rough estimates or tiered ranking (low/med/high) help.

4. Calculate the opportunity cost

Use this logic: *Opportunity cost = Value of next best option – Value of chosen option.*

If the opportunity cost is high, it signals a poor trade-off.

5. Make trade-offs explicit

Say it out loud or write it down: "If I do this, I'm giving up that."

This is where Border's screwed up. They didn't bring the intangible losses into the equation. For example, how much is customer loyalty worth?

Related Frameworks

- Opportunity Cost is one aspect of the larger model of Scenario Planning, which looks at all aspects for multiple possible futures.
- When assessing Opportunity Costs, be aware of the common tendency of Loss Aversion. People fear losses more than they value equivalent gains.
- Other people can affect your cost calculations. Use Game Theory to anticipate competitors' actions and reactions to strategic moves.

"Doing one thing means not doing another. Opportunity cost is real, and ignoring it is a hidden strategy killer." – *Clayton Christensen*

Chapter 20
Second-Order Thinking

When the COVID-19 pandemic began, Airbnb faced a sudden collapse in bookings. Its *first-order problem*—most immediate and obvious consequences—was cash flow and a flood of customer cancellations. A first-order solution would have been to retain as much cash as possible, perhaps by denying full refunds. But that's not what CEO Brian Chesky did. He chose to refund guests and compensate hosts to the tune of $250 million. This hit the company's finances hard.

Then why did Chesky do that? He was thinking further into the future, sometimes called *second-order thinking*. Someday COVID would end. Those guests and hosts would likely have long memories, and he wanted them back. Chesky was more focused on:

- Protecting long-term trust in the Airbnb platform.
- Retaining host loyalty (their supply side) to prevent competitors from gaining an edge in the future.

- Building a reputation for integrity during the crisis.

This decision garnered goodwill from both hosts and guests, and it maintained the brand's trust-based network. As the pandemic ended and as travel rebounded, Airbnb returned to profitability more quickly than many expected, successfully going public in late 2020.

What is the problem?

Most people and organizations rely on first-order thinking. They can easily see the immediate outcome of a problem or solution. This approach often leads to:

- Short-term gains that cause long-term damage
- Quick fixes that ignore root causes
- Reactions without thinking through the systemic impact
- Decisions that optimize today but undermine tomorrow

What is the Second-Order Mental Model?

Second-order thinking is a mental model used to anticipate the indirect, delayed, and non-obvious consequences of decisions or actions.

It forces you to go beyond the immediate result and consider the chain reaction your choice might trigger across time, stakeholders, and systems. Second-order thinking involves evaluating the consequences of consequences.

Instead of stopping at "What will happen because of this decision?", you ask: "And then what?" "What happens because that happened?" "What will others do in response?" "What could happen in six months, not just six minutes?"

It's like playing chess: if white makes that move, where will black go? And then what?

A Real Business Example: McDonald's in Russia

In 2022 after Russia invaded Ukraine, McDonald's made a bold move: it shut down all 850 of its restaurants in Russia, a market that had contributed over $2 billion in annual revenue.

Their first-order thinking response might have been: "Protect revenue. Stay neutral by staying silent. We don't do politics."

But McDonald's CEO Chris Kempczinski asked second-order questions: "What's the cost to our brand if we stay? How will employees, customers, and investors view our values over time? What is the long-term impact?"

So, McDonald's exited Russia completely. They sold their restaurants to a local operator, who rebranded them to protect the McDonald's name. However, they retained the option to return in the future under different conditions.

The result can be seen today. McDonald's gained a massive global reputation for taking a values-driven stand, and customer loyalty in Western markets increased. They avoided any long-term reputational risks and political complications. Employees, especially in Western Europe, expressed pride in the company.

Key Takeaways

- First-order thinking is linear and reactive.
- Second-order thinking is nonlinear and proactive.
- You should think in decision chains: Don't just stop at "What happens next?" Ask, "And then what?"

How to Apply the Second-Order Mental Model

Steps to apply second-order thinking:

1. Identify the first order consequence

Ask: "What happens immediately if I make this decision?" This is the apparent result most people stop at.

For example, if a grocery chain cuts prices, the first-order consequence is more customers and higher sales volume.

2. Ask: "Then what?"

Ask repeatedly: "What happens next? What are the ripple effects?"

In our grocery chain example, second-order effects could be: Lower prices might reduce profit margins, which would cause pressure to cut costs. Cutting costs would probably create lower quality, and then our brand would suffer.

Ask "And then what?" until you expose downstream risks and opportunities.

3. Consider multiple stakeholders

Think through how your decision affects not just you but also customers, employees, competitors, regulators, etc. For example, if you automate customer service, what's the long-term impact on your brand experience, job satisfaction, or customer loyalty?

4. Look at different time horizons

What are the outcomes over the short, medium, and long terms? What might seem like a win today could become a loss tomorrow. Buying low-quality parts may save money this quarter, but create a reputation crisis next year.

5. Compare the trade-offs

Use a decision tree or branching scenario map. Play out:

- Best-case
- Most likely case
- Worst-case outcomes

This helps surface *unexpected downsides* and *hidden upsides*.

Related Frameworks

- Divergent and Convergent Thinking can be used to help you identify second-order outcomes.
- Recognizing Confirmation Bias or pursuing information that supports existing beliefs can distort your second-order thinking.
- If your problem involves competitors, you should use Game Theory to anticipate how their actions could affect your second-order results outcomes.

"You must think in terms of second- and third-order consequences. Don't just look at the immediate results. Think through the effects of those effects." – *Ray Dalio, founder of Bridgewater Associates*

Chapter 21
Scenario Planning

NOW,
THE "TOYPOCALYPSE"

FUTURE

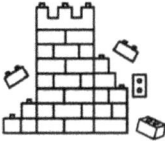

SCENARIOS

"Toypocalypse!" That's how one executive at Lego described the company's situation.

In 2003 Lego Group was in crisis. Sales were plummeting, kids were shifting to video games, and the toy manufacturer had drifted from its core. The Danish company was losing nearly a million dollars a day in 2003.

Most enterprises in this situation would focus on short-term fixes. Instead, Lego's leadership asked: "What could the future look like—not just one future, but several?"

They ran scenario planning exercises with futurists, child psychologists, and technologists. One scenario explored a world where digital and physical play merged, and another imagined open-source creativity where fans co-created new sets.

These scenarios seemed far-fetched at the time, but Lego used them to make bold decisions:

- Anticipating a world where STEM education, coding, and hands-on learning would intersect, they launched Lego Mindstorms (a robotics kit),
- Seeing online collaboration coming, they created Lego Ideas (crowdsourced set designs).
- They embraced collaborations like *Minecraft* and *Star Wars*.

Drawing from various envisioned futures, these bets propelled Lego to become the world's most valuable toy company by 2015.

Lego didn't "predict" the future. It planned for multiple futures and used those visions to stress-test decisions. That's the essence of scenario planning: building resilience, not certainty.

What is the problem?

Most leaders plan for what they believe will be "the most likely" future. But what if that future never comes? In our complex world, change can arise from unexpected sources.

You may be blindsided by economic shifts, technological disruptions, or geopolitical changes. Furthermore, leaders often prefer information that confirms their worldview and dismiss what contradicts it (confirmation bias).

"The purpose of looking at the future is to disturb the present."
– *Gaston Berger, French futurist and early advocate of scenario thinking*

What is the Scenario Planning Mental Model?

Scenario Planning is a mental model that prepares you to anticipate and respond to various plausible futures, not just the most likely one. Instead of predicting a single outcome, scenario planning explores multiple, diverging possibilities to test strategies and identify opportunities or vulnerabilities under different future conditions. This model is especially compelling when operating in high-uncertainty, high-impact environments like that of today.

A Real Business Example: Shell Oil Company

In the early 1970s, Royal Dutch Shell began using **Scenario Planning** to envision futures beyond standard projections. One scenario examined the possibility of a significant oil supply disruption. When the 1973 oil embargo struck, triggered by OPEC's decision to cut supply, Shell was one of the few oil companies ready for the shock. It had already modeled a future with a constrained oil supply and had contingency plans, such as rebalancing supply chains and investments. As a result, Shell adapted more swiftly than its competitors and climbed in global market rankings.

Key Takeaways

- Think in possibilities, not predictions. **Scenario Planning** doesn't forecast; it prepares. It broadens your mental bandwidth for complex, ambiguous futures.
- Reduce surprises and increase agility. People who regularly engage in **Scenario Planning** tend to respond more quickly and with greater confidence during crises.
- **Scenario Planning** combats overconfidence and confirmation bias. By deliberately constructing alternate futures, you challenge assumptions and prevent groupthink.

How to Apply the Scenario Planning Mental Model

To apply the scenario planning mental model effectively, you don't need to be a futurist. You just need to be willing to think in plural futures rather than betting on a single outcome.

A step-by-step guide to put it into action:

115

1. Define the key issue or decision. Begin with a strategic question: "What strategic choices do we need to make in the next six to thirty-six months that could be impacted by outside forces?" For example: "Should we invest in a new retail model as consumer behavior changes after the pandemic?"

2. Identify the major drivers of change or external forces that could affect your issue. Organize them into categories: an easy way to do this is to examine your situation through an "environmental scan." These are the typical perspectives of such a scan.

- Political (e.g., regulations concerning sustainability)
- Economic (e.g., economic downturn)
- Social (e.g., consumer preference for experiences versus products)
- Technological (e.g., AI integration in retail)
- Legal (e.g., regulations concerning sustainability)

3. Identify the two or three most uncertain and highly impactful forces. These will serve as the axes for your scenarios. Ask "What if?" questions.

For example: "What if consumers revert to in-store shopping or remain digital-first?"

"What if inflation decreases discretionary spending?"

- Create two to four distinct scenarios. Develop credible future scenarios based on combinations of how those uncertainties may unfold. Each scenario should:
  o Be internally coherent, meaning no contradictions and the "if this, then that" logic holds up.
  o Makes sense when you explain it to others.

It's also a good idea to name the scenarios (e.g., Frugal Future, Digital Surge, Green Rebellion).

5. Test your strategy. For each scenario:

- Ask: "What would our current plan look like in this context?"
- Highlight any opportunities, risks, and strategic shifts. Establish early warning indicators to determine which scenario might be emerging.
- Create contingency plans for each scenario.

Related Frameworks

- If your **Scenario Planning** involves other players, such as competitors, then you'll want to use **Game Theory**.
- In your **Scenario Planning**, you should remain aware of **Bezos's Two-way Doors** and which actions are reversible.

"Scenarios are not predictions. They are tools for ordering one's perceptions." – *Pierre Wack, former head of scenario planning at Shell*

Chapter 22
Probabilistic Thinking

Annie Duke was the winner of the 2004 World Series of Poker Tournament of Champions. She has a deep understanding of decision-making under uncertainty. As a professional poker player turned business consultant, she offers a brilliant real-world example of **Probabilistic Thinking** in action.

In a high-stakes poker tournament, Annie made a bold move: she went "all-in" with a strong hand. But she lost a lot of money. Spectators criticized her for making a poor decision. They were wrong.

Here's the twist: she did make the right decision based on the probabilities. Her odds of winning that hand were around eighty percent. But poker, like life, is messy. That means Annie Duke would still lose once every five times. Instead of judging decisions based on outcomes, Annie learned to judge them based on process. "Did I consider the probabilities? Did I weigh the risks? Yes."

Later in her consulting work, she has advised executives and start-ups to make decisions using the same model:

- Don't ask only, "Did this work?"
- Instead, ask: "Did we make the best decision *given what we knew* at the time?"

Companies often kill projects or blame teams when outcomes go south, *even if the original bet was smart.*

What is the problem?

Most people default to binary thinking: right vs. wrong, success vs. failure, safe vs. risky. This leads to poor decisions because it ignores uncertainty, overweighs outcomes, and clings to false certainty. As a result, people:

- Misjudge the quality of decisions based on outcomes (outcome bias)
- Avoid taking smart risks because they fear failure (**Loss Aversion**)
- Fail to update beliefs as new evidence appears (**Bayesian Updating**)
- Think in terms of absolutes instead of likelihoods
- Treat all decisions as if they should be "sure things."

In short: People confuse luck with skill, certainty with confidence, and success with wisdom.

"You can be wrong and still make a good decision. You can be right and still make a bad one." – *Annie Duke*, author of *Thinking in Bets*

What is the Probabilistic Thinking Mental Model?

Probabilistic Thinking is the practice of making decisions based on the likelihood of various outcomes rather than certainties.

It requires evaluating scenarios through the lens of statistical probability, assigning relative weights to different possibilities, and updating those estimates as new information emerges.

This model helps you move beyond binary thinking (success/failure, right/wrong) and instead consider a spectrum of potential outcomes, each with its chance of occurring.

Real Business Example: Lloyd's of London and the Titanic (1912)

When the *Titanic* set sail in 1912, it was hailed as "unsinkable." But behind the confidence was a more grounded, probabilistic approach by the insurers at Lloyd's of London, the world's oldest insurance marketplace.

Despite the marketing hype, insurers at Lloyd's did not assume the *Titanic* was risk-free. They understood:

1. Even the best-designed ships could face unknown risks (like human error, acts of God, and icebergs).
2. The route across the North Atlantic in April was statistically dangerous.
3. There was a non-zero probability that a major accident could occur, even if unlikely.

So, they set the insurance premium for the Titanic at £7,500 (a large sum then), insuring the ship for £1 million—about $150 million today.

When the Titanic sank, Lloyd's paid out in full. Although it was a financial blow, it was not a death sentence because they had priced the risk probabilistically, diversified their exposure, and held sufficient reserves. This was probabilistic thinking at work:

- Not outcome-based: They didn't assume the Titanic was 100 percent "safe" just because everyone else said so.

- They used base rates, taking into account how often other large, well-built ships had historically experienced issues.
- Managed tail risk: They prepared for low-probability, high-impact disasters. Spread risk among underwriters: Thus, no single party faced catastrophic loss.

This thinking wasn't about fear. It was about rigorous thinking, math, and humility in the face of uncertainty.

Key Takeaways

- Expectations matter more than certainty: Base decisions on odds and probabilities rather than the illusion of certainty.
- Anticipate a range of outcomes: Think in terms of distributions. What's the best case, worst case, and most likely scenario?
- Update beliefs with new information: Use **Bayesian Learning**. Probabilistic thinkers, like poker players, revise their assumptions as the environment evolves or the cards are revealed.
- Quality vs. outcome: A good decision can result in a bad outcome if the odds were simply against you—and vice versa.

How to Apply the Probabilistic Thinking Mental Model

Here is a step-by-step approach to applying **Probabilistic Thinking**

1. Don't think in terms of "Will this work?" Instead, consider the odds or probabilities.

Guard against using binary questions like:

- "Will this product succeed?" Instead ask:

- "What's the probability of success? What are the odds of failure? What's the expected upside vs. downside?"

To do this right, use the Expected Value tool:

Expected Value = (Probability of success × Gain) – (Probability of failure × Loss)

2. Think in terms of scenarios and ranges, rather than absolutes. Ask:

- "What's the best-case, worst-case, and most likely scenario?"
- "What is your confidence range of outcomes?"

For example, a marketing campaign might increase sales by two to ten percent. Build your forecast around that range, rather than a fixed number.

3. Use base rates (Outside View)

Before assuming your situation is unique, ask:

- "What typically happens in similar cases?"
- "What's the historical probability of success? (This is the Lloyd's of London approach.)
- This grounds your assumptions in historical reality.

4. Update your beliefs as new information emerges (**Bayesian Learning**)

Look for any indication that your assumptions should change. If new data emerges that contradicts your earlier view, don't double down—update. Ask: "Does this new information increase or decrease the likelihood of my original outcome?"

5. Avoid outcome bias

Don't judge a decision only by its outcome. Instead, ask: "Given what I knew at the time, was it the right call?"

This is critical in leadership, hiring, and investing, where luck and randomness often mask decision quality.

6. Use probabilities to guide risk management. Assign risk levels to each outcome, then:

- Hedge when the probability × downside is significant.
- Take action when probability × upside is compelling.

This helps you take calculated risks instead of avoiding them altogether.

For example, applying this in business, let's assume you're hiring a new sales representative. You assess the following probabilities:

- Best-case: 25% chance they triple your revenue.
- Most likely: 50% chance they maintain or slightly improve.
- Worst-case: 25% chance they damage morale or underperform.

So you now can weigh the potential upside against the probability and cultural risk, as well as the financial cost. A smart move will be to hire the salesperson, but hedge with a trial period or performance-based contract.

This reflects a key mental shift from "This will definitely work" to "This has a 60% chance of working. Let's prepare for the 40% where it doesn't."

Related Frameworks

- Anchoring Bias can skew our thinking by letting information set a mental "anchor."
- Confirmation Bias is being aware of the tendency to seek information that confirms existing beliefs and countering it.
- People fear losses more than they value equivalent gains. This Loss Aversion can bias our probability estimates.

"Probability is the very guide of life." – *Cicero, Roman philosopher*

Part V: Dynamic Environments

Chapter 23
Say Three, Pick One

A four-man US Navy SEAL team, specializing in sea, air, and land operations, was on a covert mission in the mountains of Afghanistan when local goat herders discovered them.

The team faced an urgent decision: What to do about the herders? They generated three options:

1. Release the herders immediately. This choice was moral and lawful, but risked the SEALs being found by the enemy, the Taliban.
2. Detain the herders and move to a new location. This would make the mission more difficult and endanger themselves and the herders. Plus, the herders would have to be released sometime.
3. Kill the herders to protect the mission and themselves. This is illegal under the Rules of Engagement and would violate the men's ethics.

After quickly weighing the consequences, the SEALs chose option #1 and released the herders. The goat herders immediately reported the SEALs to the Taliban, who soon attacked. Three SEALs were killed; only SEAL Marcus Luttrell survived. Luttrell wrote about the experience in the book *Lone Survivor*, which was also made into a movie.

What is the problem?

When faced with a problem under stress, you become susceptible to what psychologists refer to as an "amygdala hijack." An amygdala hijack occurs when the emotional part of your brain (specifically the amygdala) overrides your rational brain (the prefrontal cortex). This results in a sudden, intense emotional decision to act that may be unwise. When your brain detects a threat (real or imagined), it triggers a "fight, flight, or freeze" response—a triad of options presented before you have time to consider your choices fully.

"Emotional self-awareness isn't a soft skill—it's survival equipment. Learning to recognize and manage amygdala hijacks is part of emotional resilience and battlefield leadership." – *Unknown instructor at Naval Amphibious Base Coronado*

What is the Say Three, Pick One Mental Model?

The **Say Three, Pick One** framework is a simple process to avoid an amygdala hijack while still making a decision rapidly. It's a structured decision-making technique where you or your team:

- Generate three distinct options for solving a problem or moving forward.
- Present all three clearly, and if time allows, list pros/cons or small justifications.
- Select one option intentionally, not by default, but by choice.

If you can't say three, you're not thinking broadly enough. If you can't pick one, you're not thinking clearly enough.

A Real Business Example: US Airways Flight 1549's Hudson River Landing

In 2009, Captain Chesley "Sully" Sullenberger's plane hit a flock of geese after takeoff from New York City's LaGuardia Airport. Both engines failed. The jet was at low altitude. Seconds mattered.

The cockpit recording shows that Sullenberger considered three immediate options:

1. He instinctively turned the aircraft toward a return to LaGuardia Airport. Then he recognized that he might not make it, and many populated buildings were in his path.
2. He asked for clearance at the smaller Teterboro Airport to the west. It was closer but risky as its New Jersey area was also densely populated.
3. He could attempt to ditch the plane into the Hudson River. This had never been accomplished. It was ultra-risky, but endangered fewer people on the ground.

He said he considered three options and chose #3, ditching into the Hudson. The crew and all 155 passengers survived.

Key Takeaways

- You need to be aware of the dangers of amygdala hijacking. *The stress from emergencies shrinks your thinking, but structured options—such as forcing yourself to consider three possible actions—expand it again.* You may feel like you don't have time to consider three options. Captain Sullenberger had seconds.
- Generate options deliberately and don't just settle for the first idea. *The first idea, while often the most obvious, may not be the best.* Saying three choices forces broader

thinking. It uncovers new angles, hidden possibilities, and better creativity emerges.

- Using the **Say Three, Pick One** framework trains your mind in adaptive thinking over time. *Creating options becomes habitual.* Over time, your brain becomes faster at spotting, framing, and evaluating choices—a decisive leadership and life advantage.

How to Apply the Say Three, Pick One Mental Model

The value of the **Say Three, Pick One** framework is its simplicity and ease of use.

Step	Action	Purpose
Say Three	Force yourself or your team to create three serious options.	To open creative thinking and ensures diversity of ideas.
Frame Them	Briefly state the pros/cons of each option.	To force awareness of tradeoffs.
Pick One	Choose deliberately.	To strengthen decision quality.

Related Frameworks

- In fast-moving situations, selecting reversible decisions as described in **Bezos's Two-way Doors** mental model is preferable.
- **Confirmation Bias** or the tendency to seek information that confirms existing beliefs can skew your thinking.

"If you have only one option, you're a prisoner. If you have two, you have a dilemma. If you have three or more, you have real choices." – *Unknown, often cited in decision-making training*

Chapter 24
OODA Loop

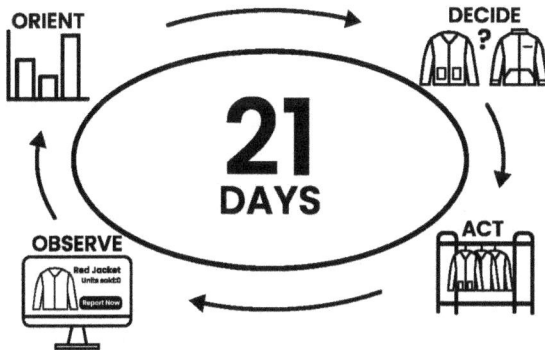

Gap (US-based) and Zara (Spain-based) are competitors. Both are global brands that sell clothing, but only one has built a retail empire by mastering the **OODA Loop**.

Gap lately has been struggling. Its supply chain has been sluggish. It takes from six to nine months to bring a new item from design to store. Meanwhile, Zara can design, manufacture, and stock a new outfit in three weeks. The difference is that Zara has embraced the **OODA Loop** framework.

Here's how Zara uses the four-step **OODA Loop** of Observe, Orient, Decide, Act:

- **Observe**: Zara store managers send daily reports about what customers are buying—or ignoring—straight to headquarters.
- **Orient**: Their teams analyze the data through a lens of real-time consumer demand, not fashion forecasting.

- **Decide**: If red jackets were selling in Milan but flopping in Berlin, they adjusted designs immediately.
- **Act**: In twenty-one days, Zara can have new stock hanging on racks. Gap typically takes that time to acquire material samples.

Zara "loops" faster than competitors. The results are clear.

Zara has experienced robust growth, whereas Gap Inc. has reported consistent declines in overall sales. Zara reported a net income that is significantly higher than Gap Inc.'s quarterly profit.

What is the problem?

Conditions shift quickly in real life, whether in combat, business, or crisis management. Many organizations and individuals struggle because they are slow to gather information, get caught in analysis paralysis, or find it challenging to adapt promptly. This results in decisions that are often made too late, too slowly, or that are too disconnected from reality.

"Zara's tight OODA loop turned supply chain into a strategic weapon—and it left slower players like Gap reeling." – *Mark Kolier* in the *Wall Street Journal*

What is the OODA Loop Mental Model?

The **OODA Loop** is a framework developed by US Air Force Colonel John Boyd. Originally intended to explain how fighter pilots could outmaneuver opponents in combat, its power extends far beyond the battlefield. It is now used in business, sports, leadership, and strategy.

At its core, the **OODA Loop** is about speed, adaptation, and clarity in fast-changing environments.

The four stages of the **OODA Loop**:

1. **Observe**: Gather data from your environment. What's happening right now? What's changed?
2. **Orient**: Analyze the information. Filter it through experience and mental models.
3. **Decide**: Choose a course of action based on your orientation.
4. **Act**: Execute the decision, then observe the results, restarting the loop.

It's not linear. Instead, it's recursive and iterative. The faster and more accurately you can cycle through the loop, the more you outmaneuver slower or less adaptable competitors.

A Real Business Example: Chick-fil-A vs. McDonald's

Chick-fil-A closely monitors its competition. They discovered that McDonald's was planning to introduce all-day breakfast on its menu. Chick-fil-A also observed a shift in customer behavior, with more individuals working irregular hours and an increase in requests for breakfast items during lunchtime. Chick-fil-A aimed to test whether these changes in consumer preferences were local or national.

They opted to gradually expand breakfast with targeted menu items (like chicken biscuits and egg-white grills). Simultaneously, they tested late-morning breakfast extensions in select markets. They implemented small, fast experiments in different regions, iterating quickly and adjusting based on real-time feedback. Meanwhile, McDonald's struggled with operational complexity (slower kitchen speeds, confused franchisees).

Then Chick-fil-A looped again and went national.

The result: Chick-fil-A's breakfast sales surged without the operational disruption that McDonald's faced. By 2020, Chick-fil-A had become the #3 fast food chain in the US by sales, despite having fewer than 3,000 stores, compared to McDonald's 13,000+ locations.

Key Takeaways

- Speed of execution matters, but only if the orientation is correct. The most critical step is orientation: biases, models, and assumptions are tested.
- You win by making quicker, more sound decisions than your competitors, completing your decision-making process before they do.
- Adaptability trumps rigidity in dynamic markets.

How to Apply the OODA Loop Mental Model

1. **Observe**: Create habits and systems to monitor what's really happening.

Ask yourself:

- What's changed in your organization, your team, or the environment?
- What are customers, competitors, or partners doing?
- What new data, signals, or patterns are emerging?

Dashboards, feedback systems, trend reports, and frontline conversations are tools that could enhance your observance.

Tip: *Don't just gather data; ensure it's relevant data, as in the Zara example. Speed without clarity is just noise.*

2. **Orient**: Interpret what your observations and data means. This is the most critical phase. I've seen companies and individuals discount data because it didn't fit their worldview or they just didn't do the work.

Ask:

- How do my assumptions shape what I see?
- What mental models, experiences, or biases are at play?

- What options do I have?

Use **Scenario Planning** or a pre-mortem to surface hidden risks or insights.

Tip: *Challenge old mental models. Your competitors are observing the same things. You can win by orienting differently.*

3. **Decide**: Now make a decision, but not one carved in stone. The **Minimum Commitment** framework can be helpful here.

Ask:

- What's the best next move, not the perfect one?
- Can you test this on a small scale before going big?
- What's the expected impact and risk?

Tip: *You may want to time-box your decision-making. Waiting too long can be just as dangerous as acting too fast.*

4. **Act**: Execute quickly and feed the next loop. Move fast. You may want to wait until you have more information or everything is double-checked. Don't.

Ask:

- What feedback are we getting immediately?
- Is it working as expected, or should we re-orient?
- Are we faster in responding than our competitors or stakeholders?

Tip: *Build feedback channels into your action, making reflection a system, not an afterthought.*

A quick summary:

Step	Mindset	Action
Observe	Awareness	Gather real-time signals
Orient	Interpretation	Analyze with mental models
Decide	Bias for action	Choose next best move
Act	Feedback > perfection	Execute, then re-loop

Related Frameworks

- When using OODA you can be prone to overcommitting resources. Keep the **Minimum Commitment Rule** in mind so that you only assign enough resources to be "in the game," while husbanding an adequate amount for other endeavors.
- When observing, don't fall prey to **Attribution Error** or attributing others' behavior to their character, but our own to external factors.
- **Bezos's Two-way Doors** model can help you identify actions that are reversible from those that are not.

"The ability to operate inside the adversary's time cycle confuses and disorients them—making it difficult for them to react effectively." – *Col. John Boyd*

Chapter 25
Goal Shedding

At Experience to Lead, a business training enterprise, the goal was rapid growth. The company had two excellent salespeople, Morgan Yeargan and Jeffery Jackson, who were actively making sales. However, their delivery and logistics teams were stretched too thin, resulting in errors and a decline in quality. Their CEO faced a decision: pursue rapid growth for quick profits or prioritize long-term customer satisfaction. The decision: instructing the sales and marketing team to halt sales. Salesperson Morgan reflected upon that year as "Ah, a painful memory!"

What's the problem?

"You can do anything, but you can't do everything" is a quote from David Allen, the author of the best-selling book *Getting Things Done: the Art of Stress-free Productivity*. As businesspeople, you may desire a lot: high quality, low costs, timely deliveries, and high morale. However, the world is full of trade-offs. The same applies to our personal lives—sometimes we have to choose between two important options, such as attending our daughter's recital or the big client meeting.

What is the Goal Shedding Mental Model?

Goal Shedding involves intentionally abandoning goals that are outdated, misaligned, or no longer relevant in order to focus resources on more meaningful or strategic objectives. Unlike failure, which implies an inability to achieve a goal, goal shedding is a conscious decision to cease pursuing something that does not serve a greater purpose. Its psychological basis includes:

- Sunk cost fallacy: Individuals often cling to goals because of previous investments of time, money, or effort, even when these goals no longer make sense.
- Cognitive load: Holding onto too many goals can cause mental strain and reduce effectiveness in achieving what truly matters.
- Identity and adaptability: As we evolve, so do our values and priorities. Goal Shedding allows us to align with a renewed vision.

"Letting go is not giving up, but accepting that there are things that cannot be." – *Unknown*

A Real Business Example: Starbucks

Howard Schultz, who once led Starbucks as CEO, returned to steer the company in 2008 when it faced significant challenges. The coffee chain had grown too quickly, introduced too many products, and lost its unique appeal. Schultz made a bold choice: He closed 600 stores that were not performing well, eliminated unnecessary items from the menu, and even shut down every Starbucks in the US for a day to retrain staff on crafting the perfect espresso. Though it was tough initially, this strategy succeeded. Starbucks emerged stronger by concentrating on its fundamental mission of delivering excellent coffee and a remarkable customer experience.

Key Takeaways

- Shedding a goal is not failure; it demonstrates strategic adaptability.
- Identifying when a goal is misaligned is a crucial leadership skill.
- Effective leaders regularly reassess priorities and make difficult decisions.
- Your goals should grow as you do.
- What was once a significant ambition may not align with your future vision.

"I have let go of many things over the years, not because they didn't matter, but because I had to make room for what mattered most." – *Chesley "Sully" Sullenberger, in Highest Duty: My Search for What Really Matters*

How to Apply the Goal Shedding Mental Model

Two types of **Goal Shedding**: Tactical and Strategic

Tactical:

Tactical goal shedding occurs during short-term execution. A person may still believe in the larger mission but recognizes that the specific step they are taking is no longer effective. In these situations, the individual releases a particular tactic while maintaining the overall goal.

For example, a student who drops a particularly demanding elective to preserve their GPA is practicing tactical goal shedding. They haven't abandoned the goal of graduating; they've simply let go of a course that would drain energy and hurt performance elsewhere. Similarly, in business, a marketing team that stops a poorly performing campaign is making a comparable move—sacrificing a tactic to conserve resources and focus on strategies with better results. Tactical shedding is practical and often situational; it demonstrates flexibility without abandoning the bigger purpose.

Strategic:

Strategic goal shedding, by contrast, involves a deeper level of change. Here, it's not just the methods that are questioned, but the end goal itself. A student who once planned to attend law school but discovers their true passion in entrepreneurship is not simply adjusting their semester's workload—they are redefining their life's purpose. The aim of becoming a lawyer is abandoned, not because of temporary setbacks, but because their broader vision has changed. Organizations do the same when they exit entire product lines or withdraw from markets that no longer align with their future. Therefore, strategic shedding is more profound and lasting. It redefines identity, redirects ambitions, and shifts the meaning of success. Together, these two types of goal shedding highlight the subtle ways humans adapt. Tactical shedding allows us to fine-tune our approach, discarding methods that no longer work. Strategic shedding, however, requires more courage because it involves recognizing when a once-cherished goal no longer fits who we are becoming. Both are essential in a world where conditions change rapidly and clarity often only emerges after the fact. Tactical shedding keeps us agile; strategic shedding keeps us true to ourselves.

Related Frameworks

- If you're in an emergency, then using the **Say Three, Pick One** mental model is an efficient way to make urgent decisions.
- If your need to shed goals is not urgent, the **Eisenhower Matrix** is an excellent way to prioritize tasks based on urgency and importance to focus on what truly matters.

- **EDAD**: or Eliminate, Delegate, Automate, Do, is a more detailed and systematic framework for reducing your decision-making workload.

"Half of wisdom is knowing what you no longer need to strive for." – *David Whyte*

Chapter 26
Eisenhower Matrix

Warren Buffett, one of the most successful investors of all time, is renowned for his disciplined approach to decision-making. He frequently speaks about how he prioritizes his time and energy.

Consider the types of matters Buffett might deal with in his daily life:

- Responding to sudden investment opportunities or legal disputes
- Handling media requests
- Building personal relationships with CEOs or potential partners
- Staying abreast of digital trends and the constant cycle of news

And so on. You get the idea.

Warren Buffett, who announced his retirement from leading

Berkshire Hathaway on May of 2025, faced the same problem as you.

What is the problem?

The challenge we face is being overloaded with daily tasks, such as emails, phone calls, and meetings—both large and small— as well as opportunities. This leads to significant stress. There always seems to be too much to do. Warren Buffett attributes much of his success to recognizing this reality and employs the **Eisenhower Matrix** to effectively prioritize his time.

"What is important is seldom urgent, and what is urgent is seldom important." – *Dwight D. Eisenhower*

What is the Eisenhower Matrix Mental Model?

It's easy to say that we should prioritize our personal and professional lives. But to do that successfully, we need a framework to guide our thinking. The **Eisenhower Matrix**, also known as the **Urgent-Important Matrix**, is a mental model designed to help individuals and teams prioritize tasks based on their level of urgency and importance. Named after US President Dwight D. Eisenhower, who was known for his efficient decision-making skills, the matrix divides tasks into four quadrants.

In World War II, Eisenhower commanded the monumental D-Day landings. This operation was the largest amphibious invasion in history, involving millions of soldiers, thousands of vessels and aircraft, and countless decisions. To manage such an overwhelming task, he established a rule that any document on his desk must be no longer than one page. This way, his Chief of Staff Walter Bedell Smith could more easily sort the documents into the four categories of the matrix. While condensing everything into one page may not always be feasible, simplifying complex issues into one of four categories remains a valuable approach:

Important

| Decide
Schedule for later | Do
Do it now |

Not Urgent ← → **Urgent**

| Delete
Eliminate it | Delegate
Who else can do it for you? |

Not Important

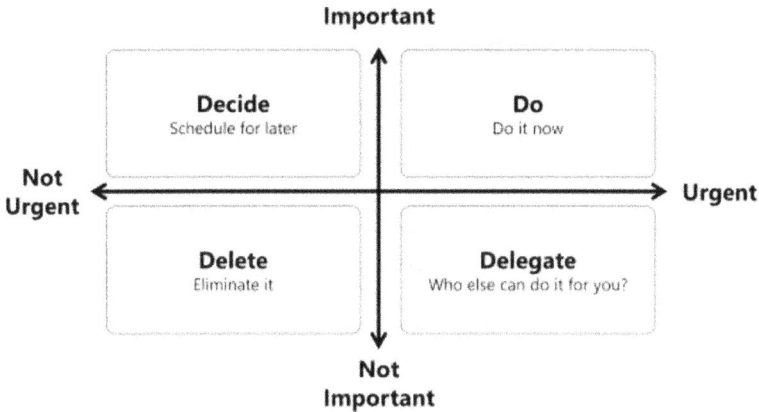

Urgent and Important: Tasks that require immediate attention and have significant consequences if not completed. Do these now! For Buffett, sudden opportunities and regulatory issues are a top priority.

"You've got to keep control of your time, and you can't unless you say no. You can't let people set your agenda in life." – *Warren Buffett*

Important but Not Urgent: Tasks that contribute to long-term goals should be scheduled intentionally. Plan or schedule when you will tackle these. Buffett sets aside time to build relationships with people and study what's important to his long-term business objectives.

"I insist on a lot of time being spent, almost every day, to just sit and think. That is very uncommon in American business. I read and think. So I do more reading and thinking, and make fewer impulse decisions than most people in business." – *Warren Buffett*

Urgent but Not Important: Tasks that require immediate action but can be handled by others should be delegated. Buffett has a staff that manages media requests and meetings.

145

"You can always make more money. You can't make more time."
– *Warren Buffett*

Neither Urgent nor Important: Tasks that add little value should be minimized or eliminated. Buffett has stated many times that he ignores media trends.

"The difference between successful people and really successful people is that really successful people say no to almost everything."
– *Warren Buffett*

If you organize your work into these categories as Buffett does, you can focus on what truly matters and avoid getting caught up in being busy without being productive.

A Real Business Example: A Non-profit Director

During coaching sessions, the owner of a small, non-profit organization discovered that he often became absorbed in tasks and issues that seemed urgent but were not truly important. He described it as being "crazy busy." He expressed that this left him with little time for strategic thinking or donor relations. However, when he began tracking his time, he realized that he spent hours on social media marketing and resolving minor software bugs. (He was a former programmer.) It became evident that browsing social media was his way of unwinding (perhaps personally important, but not urgent), and the inventory system had been operating with minor glitches for over two years without leading to any significant problems (neither urgent nor important).

When he began using the **Eisenhower Matrix**, he prioritized his tasks and delegated more effectively. Initially, it required discipline to use the matrix consistently, but it eventually became second nature to him. He had truly internalized this method when he canceled a meeting, recognizing that while the potential discussion was important, it was not urgent, and he needed to reschedule.

146

When describing the **Eisenhower Matrix**, some authors don't realize that it includes a "delete" section. Many management experts emphasize getting everything done. However, one of the most effective ways to accomplish tasks is by eliminating unnecessary ones. We may feel productive when we handle it all, but the **Eisenhower Matrix** compels us to ask the difficult questions: Do I actually need to do this? Is this task going to help me attain my vision? Will this effort benefit my long-term goals?

Key Takeaways

- Not all urgent tasks are important. Your sense of urgency can create emotional pressure and cause you to focus on the wrong things.
- Many urgent tasks are trivial.
- Importance relates to long-term goals, values, and impact.

How to Apply the Eisenhower Matrix Mental Model

Use the four quadrants to create clarity in decision-making.

Quadrant	Category	Action	Examples
1	**Urgent & Important**	Do Now	Crises, deadlines, health emergencies
2	**Not Urgent but Important**	Schedule	Strategic planning, exercise, learning
3	**Urgent but Not Important**	Delegate	Interruptions, meetings, routine emails
4	**Not Urgent & Not Important**	Eliminate	Social media scrolling, distractions

Regularly assess your work to identify what is truly important and urgent. By doing so, you can avoid the trap of merely working harder instead of smarter. You can use the **Eisenhower Matrix** with your team to assess their priorities and align with your goals.

Use the **Eisenhower Matrix** to help you reduce life's pressures and reduce stress.

Related Frameworks

- Once you've prioritized your work, you can use the **Eliminate, Delegate, Automate**, Do model to reduce the work that you have to do.
- Even after you've prioritized your tasks, it may be hard to get started on the big jobs. Use the **Franklin Framework** using micro-prioritization to get things done.

"The harder I work, the behinder I get." – *Unknown*

Chapter 27
Bezos's Two-Way Doors

By the late 2000s, Domino's Pizza faced a significant problem: customers disliked the taste.

In 2009, consumer surveys ranked their pizza near the bottom, with reviews stating it tasted like "cardboard with ketchup." Brand trust was eroding, and sales remained flat.

Domino's made two very different sets of decisions to address these issues. First, they made a bold, irreversible choice: they completely overhauled their pizza recipe. They examined everything from crust to sauce to cheese. They slowed down, tested extensively, and built prototypes. They had to perfect their core product since they knew they only had one chance at rebranding. Then they announced it to the world through a massive ad campaign. "We heard you. Our pizza sucked. We fixed it."

As those ads ran, there was no going back. But it worked. Their transparency about their product overhaul became a case study in courage.

And that's not all. As they overhauled their product, they also tested several smaller, easily reversible ideas, including:

- A real-time "Pizza Tracker"
- AI voice ordering
- Self-driving delivery tests
- Ordering from a smart TV

If any of these tests failed, the team could pull the plug with minimal risk involved. Teams were empowered to test and learn quickly, fostering a culture of experimentation and renewal. A sufficient number of these tech-forward decisions succeeded, allowing Domino's to distinguish itself as a modern digital-first food company. By combining the bold "one-shot" rebrand with the "fail fast" agile approach, Domino's became the #1 pizza chain in the US and tripled its stock price.

What's the problem?

As humans, we often treat every decision as if it were high-stakes and irreversible. This mindset can result in slow decision-making, fear of failure, and a reluctance to take risks. In fact, many decisions are not irreversible.

"Organizations that treat every decision like a Type 1 decision are like drivers slamming the brakes on every green light." – *Adam Grant*

What is Bezos's Two-Way Doors Mental Model?

In his 2015 Amazon Letter to Shareholders, Jeff Bezos outlined his framework of decision types. He used the metaphor of doors: some doors lock behind you after you use them, while others swing both ways, like the doors to the kitchen in a restaurant.

Type 1 Decisions: One-Way Doors

"These are consequential and irreversible or nearly irreversible—one-way doors. You walk through and can't go back." – *Jeff Bezos*

- Require slow, deliberate, high-quality decision-making
- Often involve big investments, acquisitions, or structural changes
- Should be made carefully, ideally by senior leaders
- Examples: Acquiring Whole Foods, launching AWS, changing business models

Type 2 Decisions: Two-Way Doors

"These are changeable, reversible—they're two-way doors. If you've made a suboptimal Type 2 decision, you don't have to live with the consequences for that long. You can reopen the door and go back through." *–Jeff Bezos 2015 Amazon shareholder letter*

- Should be made quickly and with less risk aversion
- Can be delegated to smaller teams or individuals
- Enable experimentation, iteration, and speed
- Examples: Product feature tests, pricing experiments, marketing channels

Why does this distinction matter?

"As organizations get larger, there seems to be a tendency to use the heavy-weight Type 1 decision-making process on all decisions. The end result of this is slowness, unthoughtful risk aversion, failure to experiment, and diminished invention." – *Jeff Bezos*

- Overusing Type 1 processes paralyzes innovation
- Mis-classifying reversible decisions leads to slow decision cycles
- Type 2 thinking is essential to agility, experimentation, and innovation

A Real Business Example: Amazon's HQ2 Decision

In November 2018, Amazon officially announced that it would build its much-anticipated second headquarters (HQ2) in Long Island City in Queens, New York. This decision followed a high-profile, year-long national competition among more than 200 cities. The new headquarters would bring 25,000 high-paying tech jobs and a $2.5 billion direct investment in NYC.

However, Congresswoman Alexandria Ocasio-Cortez (AOC) led the cause to gain more concessions from Bezos. She rallied community leaders and civic groups. "We're giving away three billion dollars in incentives for what? For Amazon to take over a community and gentrify it?"

She assumed that such a huge announcement was a Type 1 decision—a one-way door. In 2019, Amazon made headlines when it reversed its decision to build in Queens. Amazon's swift withdrawal reflected Type 2 decision-making—a reversible choice that could be undone without compromising the company's long-term strategic position.

Key Takeaways

- Don't treat every decision like it's life or death. Save your strategic firepower for the one-way doors. Move fast on the rest.
- Classify decisions early. Ask: Is this reversible?
- Slow down for Type 1 decisions. Use thorough analysis, consensus, and strategic foresight.
- Speed up Type 2 decisions. Empower teams to test, learn, and pivot without red tape.

"If you're good at course correcting, being wrong may be less costly than you think, whereas being slow is going to be expensive for sure." – *Jeff Bezos, 2016 Amazon Letter to Shareholders*

How to Apply Bezos's Two-Way Door Mental Model

Step 1: Ask the reversibility question

Can this decision be easily reversed if it doesn't work out?

- If yes, then go to Step 2
- If no, then treat the decision as a "One-Way Door" Type 1 Decision
  - Slow down
  - Use analysis, risk review, and leadership consensus
  - Treat the decision as a strategic commitment

Step 2: Ask the consequence question

What is the scale of impact if this goes wrong?

- Low to moderate → Type 2 Decision: Two-Way Door
  - Make it fast
  - Empower the team
  - Learn and iterate quickly
- High risk, high visibility → Re-evaluate—possibly Type 1

Step 3: Decide who should decide

Who has the knowledge, context, and agility to act on this?

- If someone is close to the problem, you probably want to delegate to them
- If it needs strategic oversight, then you need to handle this

Step 4: Default to action bias (for Type 2)

If the downside is minimal and reversible, make the call fast.

- Encourage experimentation
- Build a culture of fast iteration and course correction
- Reward speed and learning, not just being right

Related Frameworks

- If you're not able to find a reversible solution, another way to mitigate your potential losses is to use a **Margin of Safety**. Building redundancy into your system can reduce risk.
- **Inversion** or thinking backward from the desired outcome to focus on how to avoid failure is another mitigating mental model.
- The **Tame and Wicked Problems** mental model is useful in identifying the type of problem you're trying to solve and to which aspects of the problem you can apply **Bezos's Two-Way** Door mental model.

"Most decisions should probably be made with somewhere around 70% of the information you wish you had. If you wait for 90%, in most cases, you're probably being slow." – *Jeff Bezos, 2016 Amazon Letter to Shareholders*

Chapter 28
Zooming In and Out

Netflix started as a mail-order video rental service. In the early 2000s in an effort to become more efficient, Netflix "zoomed in on"—intensely focused in on and embraced—the mechanics of DVD rentals. The intent was to optimize mailing speed, return processes, and warehouse operations to improve the customer experience and reduce costs. By 2007, Netflix concluded that it had reached the point of diminishing returns on operational efficiency. The company leadership under Reed Hastings then zoomed out, looking at the broader technological landscape. They observed three things:

1. Broadband internet service was expanding rapidly, and costs were declining.
2. Consumers wanted even faster access to media than Netflix could provide.
3. The cost and inconvenience of physical media would eventually limit scalability.

This big-picture thinking led to a bold pivot into streaming long before it became the norm. In fact, Netflix's mailing service continued to generate more revenue than streaming for five years. That revenue funded the transformation into the streaming service it is today.

What is the problem?

Two common pitfalls occur during problem-solving: getting lost in details and missing the trend (micro myopia), or staying too abstract and failing to execute (macro float).

"Vision without execution is hallucination. Execution without vision is random motion." – *Thomas Edison*

What is the Zooming In and Out Mental Model?

The **Zooming In and Out** mental model is a thinking technique used to shift perspective between the big picture and the fine details of a problem, situation, or decision. It serves as a cognitive lens-switching tool, helping you strategically survey the landscape and tactically inspect the terrain.

When *Zooming In*, you want to focus on the details. It's most appropriate when you:

- Are doing process improvement, as in the case of Netflix
- Want to diagnose specific problems
- Are refining execution or tactics
- Need a granular understanding

Some examples include:

- A software engineer debugging a single line of code
- A writer editing a paragraph word by word
- A leader analyzing customer feedback comments individually

When *Zooming Out*, you want to see the big picture. It's used to see the forest instead of the tree. Zoom out when you:

- Are looking for patterns in processes or human behavior
- Need a strategic overview
- Are evaluating context, trends, or long-term implications
- Want to make higher-order decisions

Examples:

- A CEO mapping a five-year strategy across global markets
- A teacher looking at the yearlong progress of a struggling student
- A policymaker assessing the systemic impact of a proposed law

A Real Business Example: Blackberry (then Research In Motion)

In the early 2000s, BlackBerry dominated the smartphone market. Professionals loved their secure email, physical keyboards, and enterprise integration. The company focused too narrowly on its core market: government and big corporate users.

When the iPhone was released in 2007, Mike Lazaridis, who co-founded BlackBerry, said, "How did they do that? It's going to collapse the network."

In response to Lazaridis's concerns, Research In Motion's CEO Jim Balsillie said:

"It's okay. We'll be fine. As nice as the Apple iPhone is, it poses a real challenge to its users. Try typing a web key on a touchscreen on an Apple iPhone; that's a real challenge. You cannot see what you type."

Balsillie remained focused on small details. By not zooming out, he missed the strategic shift from secure communication devices to multifunctional platforms.

Key Takeaways

Zooming both in and out prevents the two classic mistakes when solving problems:

- Too much zoom in can cause getting lost in the weeds, optimizing details that may not matter.
- Too much zoom out can cause you to stay thinking in the abstract and miss key execution flaws or user pain points.

Dual thinking (zooming in and out) is smart thinking.

- Zooming in helps you understand problems at a granular, operational level.
- Zooming out helps you see the strategic context, patterns, and long-term implications.
- Great leaders toggle between both modes fluidly.

How to Apply the Zooming In and Out Mental Model

Zooming In and Out is about asking the right questions of yourself and of others.

Use these questions when you need to **Zoom Out** to get the big picture:

- What's the real problem we're solving?
- How does this fit into your larger mission or long-term goals?
- What are the broader forces or trends at play?
- What will matter five years from now?
- What would this look like from a 30,000-foot view?

Use these questions to **Zoom In** to solve tactical execution-type problems:

- What's not working right now?
- Where, when, and how are we seeing the problem or issue?
- What does the data tell us?
- Who exactly is impacted, and how?
- What is the next step we can take today?

Related Frameworks

When approaching tactics or strategy, getting the facts straight is important. The **Six Honest Serving Men** model provides a straightforward framework for uncovering the facts.

The **Pareto Principle (80/20 Rule)** is a tool to help you focus on the 20% of actions that deliver 80% of the results.

First Principles Thinking is breaking problems down into fundamental truths and reasoning up from there, instead of relying on assumptions. It's the best mental model when Zooming In.

"The art of thinking is the art of being able to zoom in and zoom out." – *Nassim Nicholas Taleb*

Chapter 29
Tame and Wicked Problems

In 2010, Boeing faced a crisis when Airbus launched the fuel-efficient A320neo, prompting airlines to rush to purchase it. To compete without developing a new plane, Boeing modified its 737 to create the 737 MAX with larger engines. Because the 737 sits low to the ground, this adjustment affected the aircraft's aerodynamics, causing the nose to pitch upward. Boeing installed new software to address this issue, which could automatically push the nose down based on a single sensor without pilot input. Boeing did not disclose this new system in training to save on simulator time. They ignored engineers who questioned the fix; instead, they focused on the schedule to surpass Airbus. In 2018 and 2019, two crashes claimed 346 lives, revealing a culture that prioritized shareholder returns over safety. The 737 MAX was grounded, severely impacting Boeing's reputation, stock, and leadership.

What is the problem?

Some problems are well-defined and, although complicated, can be solved. Others are more complex, and traditional solutions won't work; they may even worsen the situation. How can you tell the difference?

"The formulation of a wicked problem is the problem." – *Horst Rittel and Melvin Webber, originators of the wicked problem concept*

What is the Wicked vs. Tame Mental Model?

The **Wicked vs. Tame** framework helps leaders distinguish between solvable problems with existing knowledge and systems (tame) versus those that are complex, unpredictable, and resistant to definitive solutions (wicked). Understanding the difference is crucial for applying the right strategies and resources. Let's establish some definitions.

Term	Definition	Attributes
Tame	A *complicated* problem with many parts that are difficult but can be solved with enough expertise	Predictable, knowable, solvable with formulas or experts
Wicked	A *complex* problem involving many interconnected parts where outcomes are unpredictable	No clear solution path, requires judgment, learning, and adaptation

A **Tame** problem might be something like implementing a new bookkeeping system.

- Involves lots of steps, dependencies, and technical know-how.
- But if you follow the project plan and use experts, it's solvable.

A **Wicked** problem could be something like transforming company culture.

- You can't force it with a checklist.
- It requires experimentation, leadership, and feedback loops.

A Real Business Example: The Opioid Crisis and Big Pharma

How should pharmaceutical companies address their role in the opioid epidemic?

Why is this a **Wicked** problem?

1. No clear definition of the problem. Many people are addicted, but is it because of over-prescription, regulatory failure, or pain management? It depends on who you ask.
2. Every solution changes the problem. Cracking down on prescriptions could increase illegal fentanyl use. Introducing safer meds and doctors may be hesitant to prescribe anything for this problem.
3. There is no point at which all parties can agree when the problem is solved.
4. There are too many complicated parts. Patients, doctors, pharma companies, the FDA, the justice system, and insurance providers are all part of the problem with competing goals.

Some of the many business decisions to be made included:

- How should Purdue Pharma market OxyContin?
- What is McKesson's role in distribution and reporting on the use of opioids? What are patient rights?
- Johnson & Johnson has numerous lawsuits and settlements pending.
- Should CVS and Walgreens be held liable for over-

dispensing?

Key Takeaways

You will know when you have a **Wicked** problem when:

- You can't clearly define where the problem starts or ends.
- There isn't a clear moment when the problem is "solved." You just get to a better or worse version.
- There's no objectively "correct" answer: just judgments, trade-offs, and opinions.
- How you frame the issue (economic? moral? political?) shapes the options you see available.

How to Apply the Wicked vs. Tame Mental Model

Determine which type of problem you have. Boeing believed they had a tame software problem. Instead, they faced a wicked problem with multiple facets. It involved systems, with the software affecting the aircraft, pilots, and other systems.

1. Tame problems need execution, not innovation. Tame problems are ideal for process improvement, optimization, and technical expertise.
2. Wicked problems require adaptive thinking. Seek the involvement and perspectives of multiple parties. These problems benefit from iterative approaches. Test every solution as an experiment. The "Fail early and fail fast" approach is appropriate.
3. Leaders should ask: "Is this problem solvable with expertise alone, or does it require learning, flexibility, and engagement with ambiguity?"

Related Frameworks

- A simple, but useful tool to use with wicked problems is the No-cost Consultant. More perspectives, especially from those less familiar with the topic, can yield surprisingly valuable insights.

- Applying the Minimum Commitment Rule to wicked problems allows you to test your solution before making a significant commitment.
- Inversion thinking or working backwards from the desired outcome will help you avoid potential pitfalls that your solutions may cause.

"Complicated systems have many moving parts. Complex systems have many moving parts that interact and change each other over time." – *Dave Snowden, creator of the Cynefin framework*

Part VI: Personal Effectiveness

Chapter 30
Self-Efficacy

In 1996 Sara Blakely was selling FAX machines door-to-door for Danka in Florida. Her company's dress code required her to wear pantyhose. Blakely disliked the appearance of the seamed foot with open-toed shoes but appreciated how the control-top model eliminated panty lines and made her body look firmer. This sparked in her an idea of hosiery without feet.

So Blakely attempted to cut the feet out of her pantyhose. But the hosiery kept rolling up her legs. After researching her concept, she pitched her idea to textile manufacturers. She was turned down by every company. Blakely persisted in the face of continual rejection.

Ultimately, a manufacturer contacted her, motivated by the support of his three daughters. Despite having limited business experience beyond her door-to-door sales background, she launched her own venture, using her credit card to buy the "Spanx" trademark. However, retailers showed little interest.

Again, she persisted. She reached out to her old friends, asking them to visit department stores to request Spanx. Neiman Marcus took the bait and began selling Spanx in seven of its stores. In 2021, Blakely sold her company for $1.2 billion.

What is the problem?

When you encounter a new or challenging situation, the biggest obstacle is often your own belief that you can't succeed. Everyone experiences some self-doubt and fear of failure. This can lead us to make poor decisions or even avoid making decisions or pursuing goals altogether.

"Whether you think you can, or you think you can't — you're right." – *Henry Ford*

What is the Self-Efficacy Mental Model?

Self-Efficacy is a concept developed by psychologist Albert Bandura. It refers to an individual's belief in their own ability to succeed in specific situations or accomplish a certain action. Unlike general self-confidence, **Self-Efficacy** is task-specific. It directly influences how people approach a specific challenge, make decisions about that challenge, and maintain effort in the face of setbacks.

A Real Business Example: Melanie Perkins

Melanie Perkins co-founded Canva, an online design platform that is now a multi-billion-dollar company. When she started, Perkins was a university student in Perth, Australia, with no background in tech start-ups or connections to Silicon Valley.

Perkins believed she could create a design tool that was simple enough for anyone to use, even without graphic design skills. Early on, she and her partner pitched to dozens of investors and got rejected repeatedly. But she kept iterating, building prototypes and refining her pitch, convinced that her idea could democratize design. Despite initial setbacks and the slow start, she trusted her ability to learn, adapt, and persuade—core aspects of **Self-Efficacy**.

Canva launched in 2013 and quickly gained traction, becoming one of the fastest-growing design platforms globally, with over 100 million users today. Perkins's self-efficacy transformed her early rejections into motivation for improvement, ultimately establishing a company that empowers creators everywhere. Perkins illustrates how self-efficacy can drive you to persist when the world says no, turning rejections into resilience and, ultimately, success.

Key Takeaways

- Self-efficacy bridges skill gaps. Perkins lacked a background in tech or design software; however, her belief in her ability to learn and adapt enabled her to continually refine her product and pitch.
- Rejection is data, not defeat. Her early investor rejections didn't diminish her belief; she viewed them as signals to improve and adjust rather than reasons to quit.
- Persistence can be your superpower. Self-efficacy enabled her to persist, transforming an idea into a successful global business despite limited resources.

How to Apply the Self-Efficacy Mental Model

1. Audit yourself. Identify similar situations where you've succeeded and already feel confident. What beliefs or past successes contribute to this? Use these as your mental anchor—a reminder that you've succeeded at this before and can do it again.

2. Break down challenges into smaller chunks. Instead of seeing problems as overwhelming, break them into smaller steps. This helps you see progress and fuels the belief: "I can handle this one piece at a time."

3. Visualize yourself succeeding. Before making a decision, imagine the successful outcome. Picture yourself navigating challenges with skill. Visualization reinforces your self-efficacy by demonstrating that success will eventually come.

4. Seek small wins. Deliberately select tasks that you know you can manage early in the process. Each small win builds momentum and enhances your self-efficacy, creating a feedback loop of confidence and growth.

5. Reframe setbacks. View setbacks not as failures but as momentary opportunities to adapt and learn. Self-efficacy increases when you see yourself as capable of adjusting your course rather than always executing perfectly.

6. Surround yourself with support. Rely on colleagues and friends for feedback and encouragement. Positive reinforcement boosts self-efficacy, particularly during complex decisions.

Related Frameworks

- **First Principles Thinking**: Breaking problems down into fundamental truths and reasoning up from there, instead of relying on assumptions.
- **Franklin Framework**: Using micro-prioritization to get things done.
- **Loss Aversion**: Understanding that people fear losses more than they value equivalent gains.

"People's beliefs about their abilities have a profound effect on those abilities." – *Albert Bandura*

Chapter 31
Minimum Commitment

In 2007, Brian Chesky and Joe Gebbia were two roommates struggling to pay rent in San Francisco. A big design conference was coming to town, and all the hotels were fully booked. They saw an opportunity. They inflated an air mattress in their living room, offered "Air Bed and Breakfast" to conference-goers, and included breakfast made by Joe. They charged $80 a night and got three paying guests.

Airbnb was born. Instead of launching a full-blown start-up with investors, engineers, and branding, they did something radically small: they inflated an air mattress in their living room. They tested one assumption: *Will people pay to stay in a stranger's home?* This illustrates the **Minimum Commitment** framework.

What is the problem?

We all have limited resources, with many ideas and people vying for our attention. Therefore, we need a strategy to manage our time and resources wisely, focusing on what yields the greatest return or satisfaction.

"How do you eat an elephant? One bite at a time." – *An old joke*

What is the Minimum Commitment Mental Model?

The **Minimum Commitment** framework is the concept that you should allocate the least amount of resources to a project or idea before committing significant time and resources. The guiding principle is to "commit only what's necessary to learn, test, or advance." The value of this approach lies in maintaining flexibility and avoiding the traps of sunk costs. It's about preventing overcommitment until the fog clears and true clarity emerges.

This mental model has roots deeply embedded in lean thinking, agile development, and experimental design. It counters our human tendencies toward overconfidence, perfectionism, and fear of missing out. In a world that idolizes hustle and often mistakes busyness for progress, this approach is both a relief and a revelation. Committing to less than you're inclined to can be surprisingly hard, but it can also be remarkably liberating.

This practice allows you to focus on experimentation, uncovering truths, and testing assumptions.

A Real Business Example: Oprah Winfrey

Oprah Winfrey has always been a reader. She pondered whether she could inspire more people to read by sharing her favorite books. Instead of starting a large-scale literacy initiative or investing in publishing, she made a small commitment: She chose a single book and told her television audience, "Let's read this together," then talked about the book on her show. There was no new platform, technology, or cost involved—just a segment on her existing program. A simple experiment. The outcome? This segment evolved into Oprah's Book Club, one of the most influential literary platforms globally. Books featured in the club create sales that soar into the millions, launching new careers and transforming lives. It now includes collaborations with Apple TV+, author interviews, and a comprehensive online community.

Key Takeaways

- Don't overcommit your time or energy. This applies to your personal life as well as your business.
- Start small to learn fast. Make the smallest possible move that allows you to test an idea or direction.
- De-risk big decisions. Break big ideas into small, low-cost experiments. This reduces fear and husbands your resources.
- Momentum > Masterpiece. If you're a young professional, you don't need perfection; you need movement. Small efforts tend to compound, for example, interest on money.
- "Kill Fast, Pivot Clean." Small commitments make it easier to stop what doesn't work.

You don't get stuck in sunk costs or ego traps.

How to Apply the Minimum Commitment Mental Model

1. Begin with an hypothesis, not a plan. Instead of diving into a large project, consider the following:

- What do I want to learn, validate, or discover?
- For example: "Will people be willing to pay for this?"
- Not: "How do I expand this to 10,000 users?"

2. Ask yourself: What's the simplest step I can take?

- Break down the idea into its most basic testable component.
- Thinking of launching a product? → Try it out with a

landing page.
- Want to write a book? → Share a short article or chapter on LinkedIn.
- Considering a coaching business? → Offer a free session to a friend.

3. Define your time and cost limits

- Set boundaries for your experiment.
- "I'll invest \$100 to try it out." Or "I'll halt if there's no progress in two weeks."
- Boundaries make you pause and assess.

Related Frameworks

- The **No-cost Consultant** mental model emphasizes seeking perspectives from others, particularly those who have limited prior knowledge about your issue. They can pose unexpected questions and help you evaluate your options.
- **Asymmetric Bets** involve seeking opportunities where the potential upside significantly outweighs the downside. These are strong candidates for the **Minimum Commitment** model.

The reason we have engagements before marriage and probationary periods in employment is to limit and test our commitment.

Chapter 32
Franklin Framework

Feeling overwhelmed? Perhaps Benjamin Franklin has the answer.

Benjamin Franklin achieved remarkable feats throughout his life:

- He invented the lightning rod, bifocals, and swimming fins.
- He founded the University of Pennsylvania and the first public library.
- He assisted in drafting the Declaration of Independence and served as US ambassador to France.
- He discovered the Gulf Stream current and was a prolific writer.

How could one man accomplish so much across such diverse fields of endeavor?

What is the problem?

If you're reading this book, you're likely a high-achieving individual. Moreover, you probably feel frustrated at times when your goals aren't met because your daily behaviors do not align with achieving them. Even high performers can get stuck when:

- They are overwhelmed by too many tasks competing for their attention.
- They act reactively instead of intentionally in their day-to-day decisions.
- Their time and energy are absorbed by what's urgent rather than what is important.

"You will never change your life until you change something you do daily. The secret of your success is found in your daily routine." – John C. Maxwell

What is the Franklin Framework Mental Model?

In academic circles, the Franklin Framework is also known as "micro-prioritization." This practice involves making rapid, high-frequency prioritization decisions about small tasks and interactions that accumulate over time. Unlike traditional prioritization, which focuses on major goals or quarterly plans, this approach generally operates on a daily schedule. It's about constantly recalibrating what matters right now, 365 days a year, to achieve long-term outcomes.

Ben Franklin was known for his disciplined daily schedule. He famously used a simple framework of daily questions that included two crucial prompts:

Morning question: "What good shall I do this day?"
Evening question: "What good have I done today?"

These straightforward yet meaningful questions anchored his day in purpose and self-reflection.

A Real Business Example: Satya Nadella at Microsoft

When Satya Nadella became CEO of Microsoft in 2014, he inherited a company riddled with internal competition and stagnation. Instead of launching massive structural overhauls and strategy changes, he began using the Franklin Framework to change the culture. He started with how meetings were run, how leaders gave feedback, and how teams collaborated.

One example: Nadella emphasized a shift from a "know-it-all" to a "learn-it-all" culture. He prioritized small daily actions like changing the language in executive meetings, rewarding curiosity, and personally modeling humility. These seemingly minor shifts, made repeatedly, reset the tone for an entire global organization. Over time, they added up to Microsoft's resurgence as a cultural and financial powerhouse.

Key Takeaways

- Attention is your most limited resource. Where you direct your focus minute by minute constitutes a direct investment in your future.
- Small choices indicate big priorities. The email you respond to first, the person you focus on, and the words you choose in feedback reveal what you genuinely value.
- Consistency matters. Micro-prioritization builds momentum. A thousand small, aligned actions outperform one big burst of effort.

How to Apply the Franklin Framework Mental Model

You are likely performing at least three tasks each day or on at least three on-going projects or focus areas, and typically the same each day. Research suggests using a lightweight structure like Ben Franklin's to make this habitual.

1. Morning: Identify your top 1-3 micro-moves that advance your goal today.
2. Hourly check-ins: Pause to ask, "Am I working on what matters most right now?"
3. End-of-day review: What did I prioritize well? Where did I drift?

Tip: *Use a calendar, whiteboard, or Post-it Note with your daily micro-moves to keep them visible at all times. They act as cues or reminders.*

Related Frameworks

- If you have difficulty deciding on which tasks you want to apply the **Franklin Framework** to, then you should consider using the **Eisenhower Matrix** to prioritize tasks based on urgency and importance.
- The **Franklin Framework** is one way to get stuff done. However, consider that some tasks can be assigned to others or even eliminated entirely by using the **EDAD— Eliminate, Delegate, Automate, Do** mental model.
- Sometimes you only want to allocate enough resources to be "in the game," while conserving your time and effort for other endeavors. The **Minimum Commitment** mental model is designed for that.

"Inch by inch, life's a cinch. Yard by yard, life is hard." – *John Bytheway*

Chapter 33
Anti-Fragility

In 2001, Tom Brady was a sixth-round draft pick, the 199th overall, and a backup quarterback for the National Football League's New England Patriots. Hardly anyone knew of him and if they did, they certainly didn't expect greatness . He sat behind veteran Drew Bledsoe, seemingly destined for obscurity.

Then chaos struck. In the second week of the season, Bledsoe took a brutal hit and suffered internal bleeding. Suddenly, Brady was thrust into the starting role. Most players in that position would have crumbled under pressure.

Brady did the opposite. He didn't just survive the stress; he thrived on it. He led the team to a Super Bowl victory that season. Over the next two decades, his New England Patriots won seven Super Bowl titles. Brady earned more championships than any player in NFL history, all while facing doubters, constant pressure, and competition.

What made Brady thrive rather than fall apart? Sports analysts stress three characteristics:

1. **Frame of mind**. Because he had been so underestimated, Tom Brady had an obvious chip on his shoulder. "That chip on his shoulder—that's his edge." – *Bill Belichick, Brady's coach*

2. **Experimentation and adaptation**. Instead of burning out, he evolved, changing his training, diet, body mechanics, and mindset, becoming more efficient and effective with age.

3. **Extreme discipline**. He used adversity (bench time, criticism, injury doubts) as fire for improvement. Brady didn't just bounce back from setbacks; he turned them into *fuel* to get better. He *needed* the doubt, the hits, the pressure. Without them, the legend wouldn't have formed.

What is the problem?

Most systems—businesses, careers, organizations—are designed for efficiency, not resilience. They can thrive in stable environments, but they break under volatility, uncertainty, stress, or shock. This makes them fragile in a world that is anything but stable. It's also true of individuals.

Some common types of fragility:

- Companies collapse after unexpected market changes. Examples are Blockbuster and Nokia.
- Leaders burn out when faced with compounded stress, as seen in Boeing and Nike.
- Supply chains disintegrate when a single link fails, exemplified by the *Ever Given* ship in the Suez Canal.
- Over-optimized systems can crumble under disruptions, such as COVID-19 shortages.

These failures stem not only from fragility but also from the illusion of stability. Traditional thinking conditions individuals to resist change rather than to benefit from it.

"You want to be that guy who, when the lights come on, the pressure's on—performs better." – *Tom Brady*

What is the Anti-Fragility Mental Model?

Anti-Fragility is a mental model developed by Nassim Nicholas Taleb. It describes systems, entities, or strategies that *gain* from disorder, stress, volatility, or disruption, unlike fragile systems, which break under pressure, or robust systems, which endure it without improving. Anti-fragile systems improve when exposed to chaos.

Think of it as the opposite of fragile. If fragility breaks under pressure and robustness resists it, anti-fragility *thrives* because of it.

A Real Business Example: Amazon

Amazon is a quintessential anti-fragile company. From its beginning, Amazon operated in a state of constant experimentation, failure, and reinvention. It exposed itself to small, frequent stressors (like launching new services, building AWS, or experimenting with Kindle and Alexa), each carrying minimal downside but massive upside if successful.

COVID-19 further demonstrated Amazon's anti-fragility. While the pandemic disrupted supply chains and traditional retailers, Amazon's decentralized logistics, cloud infrastructure (AWS), and culture of innovation allowed it to scale rapidly. Net sales increased by thirty-eight percent, reaching $386.1 billion in the first year of the lockdown. It didn't just survive the chaos; it expanded, hiring hundreds of thousands of workers and increasing its market share dramatically.

Key Takeaways

- Don't try just to survive or resist change and disruption. Instead, think about how you can use it to your advantage.
- Prepare yourself mentally to step up in times of chaos.
- In business, decentralization prevails. Flexible, distributed systems are less likely to fail and more likely to adapt.
- Don't overfocus on optimization at the cost of resilience. Lean systems may be "efficient" but fragile. Anti-fragile systems build in redundancy and optionality.

How to Apply the Anti-Fragility Mental Model

The first step is mental preparedness.

Bob Eckard, the former CEO of Mattel, ended every staff meeting with a question. He'd ask one person a "what if?" question. "What if the teamsters went on strike?" "What if one of the executives had a scandal?" "What if a plant had a fire?" But he wouldn't ask that of a person who had that job. He'd ask an unrelated manager. It was to keep his team thinking in terms of contingencies and how to handle them to the company's advantage.

Use redundancy to absorb shocks.

Over-optimized systems are fragile. Redundancy is a buffer against the unexpected. You could build cash reserves or surplus inventory. Cross-train employees so your organization isn't reliant on a single person. Have multiple suppliers or vendors. Redundancy may seem inefficient, but it's an investment in survival and agility.

Train under pressure to create controlled discomfort.

Anti-fragile systems strengthen under stress. Intentionally simulate high-pressure scenarios (e.g., fire drills, leadership stress tests). Practice difficult conversations and decision-making in uncertain contexts. Use stretch goals that require adaptation and

182

learning. Like muscle under resistance, capability grows with challenge.

Debrief everything.

Organizations that must be anti-fragile, such as NASA and the military, debrief nearly everything they do. This fosters a culture of rapid feedback loops. Anti-fragile systems evolve by learning quickly from failure. Encourage prompt feedback from customers, users, or teams. Reward intelligent risk-taking and experimentation, even when it doesn't succeed. Fail small. Learn fast. Adapt faster. Build optionality.

Having multiple pathways and options fosters agility, and agility is anti-fragile. Don't lock into one career path or strategy. Instead, focus on building transferable skills. Design business models with multiple revenue streams. Maintain flexible capital and bandwidth to capitalize on sudden or unexpected opportunities.

Related Frameworks

- Updating your beliefs and probabilities based on new evidence using **Bayesian Learning** can help you become more anti-fragile.
- The **Circle of Control and Circle of Influence** mental model can help you be more aware of what you can and cannot control or influence.
- **Game Theory**—anticipating competitors' actions and reactions can force you to be more flexible and resilient.

"I was cut from my high school basketball team. I've failed over and over and over again in my life. And that is why I succeed."
– *Michael Jordan*

Chapter 34
Bayesian Learning

When Procter & Gamble (P&G) launched their new air freshener Febreze, they believed it would be a smash hit. They expected that consumers would use it to eliminate bad odors—especially in homes with pets or smokers.

But early sales were disappointing. So what did P&G do? Instead of doubling down on their original belief, they questioned their own assumptions.

They believed that people would use Febreze to eliminate bad smells. Febreze was a product of P&G's Fabric and Home Care Division. They checked their assumptions with sensory scientists in the food and cosmetics division. They found that people often can't smell their own odors (olfactory fatigue), and those who could were ashamed to admit they needed it.

P&G updated its assumptions and beliefs. They changed their marketing. They relaunched the product focusing on "positive

185

habit loops and emotional rewards" and not on the negative message of bad odors. New ads repositioned Febreze as the "finishing touch" in a cleaning ritual. Ads showed happy people spraying Febreze after tidying up a room—not because it stunk, but because it felt fresh and satisfying.

Sales skyrocketed, and Febreze evolved into a billion-dollar brand. Its success can be attributed to P&G's willingness to seek new knowledge and to question their assumptions.

What is the problem?

We tend to make decisions based on fixed beliefs, even when new evidence contradicts those beliefs. This includes several cognitive failures discussed in this book, such as clinging to our initial beliefs (anchoring bias), ignoring disconfirming evidence (confirmation bias), and failing to clearly define what our beliefs actually are.

In short, we struggle to adjust our beliefs in response to new, incomplete, or evolving evidence.

"When the facts change, I change my mind. What do you do, sir?" – *John Maynard Keynes*

What is the Bayesian Learning Mental Model?

Bayesian Learning is an aid to problem-solving and decision-making that helps update our beliefs incrementally. It stems from Bayes' Theorem, a mathematical formula used to calculate the probability of a hypothesis being true given prior knowledge (the prior) and new evidence (the likelihood).

It's not about jumping to conclusions. It's about adjusting beliefs rationally as reality unfolds—one data point at a time. The key is to look for incremental changes in our assumptions.

A Real Business Example: Netflix's Gradual Shift to Streaming

186

In the mid-2000s, Netflix was primarily known for its DVD rental-by-mail service. However, Reed Hastings and his executive team noticed early signs of digital streaming adoption and declining DVD demand. Rather than waiting for overwhelming proof, they updated their internal belief about the future of media bit by bit as bandwidth improved, smart TVs emerged, and consumer interest shifted.

In 2007, streaming accounted for less than one percent of the movie-rental business. But Netflix saw early evidence: user behavior, broadband growth, and device compatibility. They gradually reallocated R&D and content licensing toward digital.

By 2011, Netflix divested its DVD business, creating "Qwikster," which failed. However, the **Bayesian** pivot continued toward content streaming. Netflix became the dominant streaming service globally by consistently adjusting its beliefs and strategies based on evolving consumer behavior and technology trends.

Key Takeaways

- All decisions begin with assumptions. Make yours clear.
- Update your beliefs, but don't overreact. New evidence should adjust, not overturn, beliefs unless it's compelling.
- Avoid dogmatism: Leaders who do not update their beliefs based on new data (e.g., Blockbuster, Kodak) risk becoming irrelevant.
- Quantify uncertainty: **Bayesian Thinking** encourages working with probabilities, not absolutes.

How to Apply the Bayesian Learning Mental Model

The first and often most challenging step is to articulate your current assumptions and beliefs. Thomas Bayes referred to this as your "Prior Belief," suggesting that it may change.

Ask yourself, "What do I currently believe about the situation?" You may want to test your thinking by discussing it with others.

Use the **No-cost Consultant** framework. Then, assign a rough probability (even if just in your head) to your assumptions.

The second step is to be on alert for new evidence from real-world outcomes, feedback, or data. Ask yourself, "Does this evidence support or challenge my belief?" Gradually adjust your assumptions. Lower or raise your confidence in proportion to the strength of new information.

Bayesian Learning is not a one-and-done proposition. It's iterative. Continue to seek new evidence and data.

Related Frameworks

- The initial information we see begins the Anchoring Bias in our minds. This anchoring inhibits our ability to accept new knowledge and learn.
- Calculating Expected Value can cause us to accept new information.
- The Minimum Commitment Rule can mitigate our actions if we're not continually adjusting our opinion, assigning enough resources to be "in the game," while preserving an adequate amount for other endeavors.

"Bayesians are people who think they ought to change their minds sometimes." – *Andrew Gelman, Columbia University statistician*

Chapter 35
Stockdale Paradox

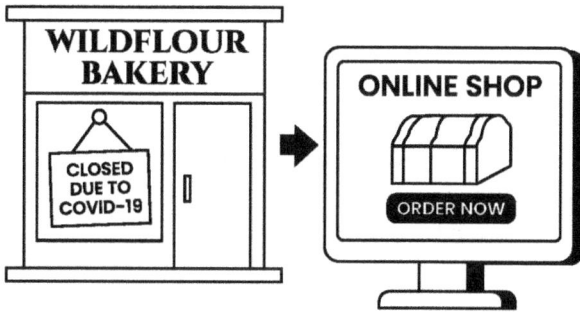

In March 2020, the global COVID-19 pandemic reached the United States. Wildflour Bakery—a beloved artisan bakery in Northern California—lost eighty percent of its revenue in a month. Tourists vanished. Farmers' markets shut down. Staff had to be furloughed.

Owner Tami Taylor's family was torn. Some were convinced the pandemic would pass as SARS did in 2003, while others believed they should shut down and cut their losses. Tami wasn't overly optimistic, nor was she a defeatist. She faced the brutal truth: the walk-in business was failing. However, she believed that people still wanted her unique products. Rather than give up, she made the following bold moves:

- She turned to online orders and prepaid subscription bread boxes.
- She partnered with local farms to co-package produce and bread.

- She personally delivered her sourdough to loyal customers within a thirty-mile radius.

By 2021, Wildflour was back in the black, and in February 2023, the store reopened.

What is the problem?

When individuals or organizations confront persistent adversity without a clear resolution, they often fall into one of two traps: (1) blind optimism, which denies reality and leads to inadequate preparation, or (2) hopeless realism, which acknowledges harsh truths but saps the will to persist. Both mindsets are perilous. One results in shattered morale when expectations are unmet, while the other leads to inaction and collapse.

"You can't romanticize your storefront when the street is empty— but you can still bet on your recipe." – *Tami Taylor*

What is the Stockdale Paradox Mental Model?

The **Stockdale Paradox** is a powerful mental model drawn from the experience of Admiral James Stockdale, a US Navy officer who was held as a prisoner of war in Vietnam for over seven years. He observed that some prisoners were blind optimists often predicting being saved by the next holiday. Others were fatalistic, accepting that they would never see freedom. Stockdale was among those few who confronted the brutal facts of their situation yet held on to an unwavering belief that they would ultimately prevail.

The **Stockdale Paradox** represents the mental agility to confront the harsh truths of your current reality while maintaining unwavering faith that you will ultimately succeed. The term was coined by Jim Collins in *Good to Great: Why Some Companies Make the Leap…and Others Don't*. This paradox serves as a mental model for resilient thinking under pressure.

190

A Real Business Example: Tristan Walker and the Razor's Edge

Tristan Walker had experienced a problem that millions of Black men face: razor bumps caused by shaving products not designed for their skin or hair type. He saw a glaring gap in the market. But when he pitched "Bevel," a high-quality razor system tailored to men of color, he was met with polite nods and cold rejections. Investors didn't get it. They didn't believe the market was big enough. Walker was a young, Black entrepreneur in a tech space that was overwhelmingly White and male. The odds were steep. Over one hundred venture capitalists turned him down.

But Tristan Walker didn't flinch. He stared those facts in the face and kept showing up. What kept him going? An unwavering belief that Black consumers deserved products made for them. He founded Bevel with start-up capital from a few individual investors. He started small, listening to customers, shipping razors himself. In 2017, he barely broke even but landed a contract with Target. In 2018, Procter & Gamble acquired Walker & Company. Tristan became the first Black CEO of a P&G subsidiary.

Key Takeaways

- Understanding the Stockdale Paradox requires dual thinking. You must face reality head-on, accepting that the problems you encounter are real, while also believing that you can ultimately succeed.
- Holding two contradictory thoughts in your mind, especially when it causes discomfort or a feeling of internal conflict, is known as cognitive dissonance. It's challenging. However, individuals who can manage this apparent incongruity are often able to navigate the toughest problems.

How to Apply the Stockdale Paradox Mental Model

When you face a difficult situation, the key is to focus on two fundamental questions:

"What's the hardest truth I need to face right now?"
"What's the deeper reason I must not give up?"

From those questions, use these steps to dig deeper:

1. Audit your current situation honestly. Use data, feedback, and difficult conversations to strip away denial. Ask: "What's really happening here?" Not what you hope is happening.
2. Clarify your "why." Why does this matter? Why is it worth enduring pain? Why is success still possible?
3. Set long-term vision anchors. Think in years, not quarters. Keep your eyes on ultimate triumph, not short-term comfort.
4. Protect the flame. Shield hope from despair, not by lying, but by focusing on progress, relationships, and purpose.

Related Frameworks

- The **Franklin Framework** is a practical method to keep taking action when progress feels most impossible.
- **Confirmation Bias** may lead you to view your situation with excessive optimism or pessimism.

"You must never confuse your faith that you will prevail in the end—which you can never afford to lose—with the discipline to confront the most brutal facts of your current reality, whatever they might be." – *Admiral James Stockdale*

Part VII: Weaving it All Together

Chapter 36
The Latticework of Models

When US Airways Flight 1549 struck a flock of geese shortly after takeoff, both engines failed. Captain Sully Sullenberger had to decide in less than four minutes how to save 155 lives. He drew upon a combination of mental models. Some were instinctive and others were consciously learned. I was on the Miracle on the Hudson and have discussed Sully's thinking with him. He used three mental models.

1. **Circle of Control** – The situation was catastrophic, but Sully immediately focused only on what was within his control and what he could influence.

- He couldn't control the bird strike. He couldn't restart the engines. And most importantly, he couldn't control the fact that he didn't have the airspeed or height to keep the aircraft in the air very long.
- He could control communication with the LaGuardia control tower, the glide angle, and the direction of landing.

- He could influence the crew and, to a lesser degree, the passengers. This mental shift prevented paralysis and channeled energy into actions that mattered.

2. **OODA Loop (Observe–Orient–Decide–Act)** – Sully had learned and practiced the OODA loop as a cadet at the US Air Force Academy and as a fighter pilot.

Sully ran this OODA cycle:

- **Observe**: Both engines out, losing altitude and momentum.
- **Orient**: Considering geography, LaGuardia was too far away, Teterboro involved flying over a populated area, the Hudson River was clear of traffic, and the water was calm.
- **Decide**: Attempt a water landing.
- **Act**: Execute precise control of descent and water contact.

His OODA loop was completed in seconds, while under extreme pressure.

3. Fast and Slow Thinking

Sully had seconds, but his training allowed him to toggle between **System 1 (fast, intuitive reaction)** and **System 2 (deliberate analysis).**

System 1 – He took control of the aircraft from co-pilot Jeff Skiles, turned on the Auxiliary Power Unit (APU), and turned south.

System 2 – He requested alternative landing options from the control tower. He turned to his co-pilot twice, asking, "Any ideas?"

He *didn't* just react. He quickly ran calculations on altitude, distance, and glide path. Training gave him "muscle memory" for fast thinking, but he layered it with slow thinking to reject the easy-but-wrong choice of turning back to LaGuardia.

Sully landed the Airbus A320 on the Hudson River. All 155 passengers and crew survived. It was hailed as the "Miracle on the Hudson," but in reality, it was a demonstration of disciplined decision-making under duress, powered by a few timeless mental models.

What is the problem?

People and organizations make poor decisions because they rely on a limited range of tools or a single mental model. They tend to prioritize perspectives from their respective fields (e.g., finance, law, engineering). This siloed thinking results in blind spots, superficial analysis, and precarious strategies.

More specifically, using one dominant framework to explain or solve everything leads to tunnel vision (e.g., viewing every business problem as a financial optimization problem). Believing your field's models are universally valid can give you a feeling of false confidence in your decisions.

"You must know the big ideas in the big disciplines and use them routinely—all of them, not just a few." – *Charlie Munger*

What is the Latticework of Models Framework?

The **Latticework of Models** is a framework about mental models—a meta-model, if you will. Popularized by Charlie Munger (Warren Buffett's business partner), it emphasizes that no single discipline has all the answers. Instead, smart decision-making requires a network (latticework) of models. This solves the problem of narrow thinking by helping you:

- Think more broadly.
- Spot non-obvious patterns and leverage points.
- Understand complex systems with nuance.

A Real Business Example: Jeff Bezos and the Kindle (2004–2007)

When Amazon set out to create the Kindle, the company entered unknown territory: hardware, digital publishing, and rights management. Bezos and his team navigated this leap not by one model, but by weaving a latticework of mental models.

1. First Principles Thinking

Bezos asked: "What do readers really want?" Instead of starting from what existed (clunky e-readers, clumsy PDFs), he broke the problem down to its essence:

- Instant access to any book ever written.
- A screen that feels like paper.
- Lightweight, portable, long battery life.

This stripped away assumptions and framed the Kindle not as a gadget but as a reading experience revolution.

2. OODA Loop (Observe–Orient–Decide–Act)

Amazon ran rapid OODA loops: testing prototypes, securing publisher deals, refining pricing, and learning from each cycle faster than competitors like Sony. Speed of iteration was key to beating incumbents.

3. Expected Value

Even though Kindle was risky and costly upfront, Bezos calculated that the long-term expected value (expanding the universe of book buyers, locking in loyalty, monetizing digital libraries) dwarfed the risks.

4. Bezos's Doors (One-Way vs. Two-Way)

Launching Kindle was a one-way door decision: once you invest billions in hardware, there's no going back. Bezos distinguished this from reversible choices (like tweaking subscription terms), ensuring they made the big decision deliberately while moving fast on the small ones.

Together, this **latticework of models** gave Amazon the clarity and conviction to reshape reading worldwide.

The Kindle, launched in 2007, sold out in 5.5 hours and changed not only Amazon but also the publishing industry itself. Today, it's a case study in how leaders who apply a latticework of mental models make bolder, smarter decisions.

Pattern recognition improves: A latticework enables you to spot analogies and patterns others overlook.

How to Apply the Latticework of Models

Step 1: Build your mental model library. This book contains foundational models from a variety of disciplines. Think of this as building a mental "toolbox."

- Psychology: **Confirmation bias, Loss aversion**
- Economics: **Opportunity cost**
- Systems Thinking: **Second-Order Thinking, First Principles Thinking**

- Math & Probability: **Bayesian Updating, Probabilistic Thinking**
- Business & Strategy: **Inversion, Pareto Principle**

Step 2: Try using different models to test which are most relevant to this problem.

Use your mental models like a checklist:

Decision Filter	Example
Opportunity cost	What am I not doing if I say yes to this?
Second-order thinking	What are the unintended consequences?
Circle of competence	Do I truly understand this area, or am I guessing?
Inversion	What would guarantee failure? How do I avoid that?

Use the right model for the right context—don't force fit.

Step 3: Keep iterating.

Your lattice framework shouldn't be fixed. That is, it grows and changes with experience. Specifically, after big wins or setbacks, ask yourself:

"What mental models did I use—and which did I miss?"

All of the frameworks mentioned in this section are either in this book or one of the three companion books in this series.

"What is elementary, worldly wisdom? Well, the first rule is that you can't really know anything if you just remember isolated facts and try to bang 'em back... You've got to have models in your head. And you've got to array your experience—both vicarious and direct—on this latticework of models." – *Charlie Munger*

Chapter 37
Cruel Sea

Nicholas Monsarrat's 1951 novel *The Cruel Sea* is a fictionalized tale based upon World War II events about British naval officers escorting merchant ships across the North Atlantic during the war. Lieutenant-Commander George Ericson must decide whether his ship, HMS *Compass Rose*, should break convoy formation during an attack in order to rescue survivors from a torpedoed merchant ship. If he does that, he endangers the convoy and the *Compass Rose*, which must stop dead in the water, thus presenting a target for a German U-boat he knows is lurking nearby. Yet Ericson orders the *Compass Rose* to circle back and pick up men in the freezing water. He is successful and saves the lives of thirty-eight sailors. His crew hails him for his humanity and heroism.

Ericson faces a similar situation days later with sailors trapped in the freezing North Atlantic. He considers rescuing them, but at the last moment his sonarman informs that a U-boat is directly beneath the struggling men. Ericson confronts a conundrum: if he attempts to save the sailors, the U-boat will likely torpedo him. If he drops depth charges to target the U-boat, the men in the water will be killed by the concussion.

Ericson orders depth charges to be dropped. This kills the sailors in the water. The sonarman then informs Ericson that the sonar's blip wasn't a U-boat after all. Ericson's crew eventually learns this and subsequently loathes Ericson. They shun any unnecessary contact with him.

What is the problem?

Similar to Ericson, some of your decisions throughout your life and career will lead to success while others will not.

"The sea has no pity, no conscience, no understanding, no compassion. Only the obligation to survive." – *Nicholas Monsarrat, The Cruel Sea*

What is the Cruel Sea Framework?

In Monsarrat's book, the ocean environment is often called "the cruel sea," but the sea is not evil. It simply doesn't care. It punishes weakness, rewards discipline and preparation, and leaves behind the careless. When we think about mental frameworks, *The Cruel Sea* serves as a reminder of any system, whether in business, warfare, or life, that:

- Luck plays a role in our success or failure.
- The system can be unforgiving and requires us to navigate skillfully.
- Success requires hard work and perseverance without any guarantees of fairness or comfort.
- We should expect uncertainty and stress.

A Real Business Example: Netflix

In the late 1990s, Netflix operated in a very "cruel sea environment."

- DVDs were still a new technology.
- Postal delivery was slow.
- Blockbuster was dominant and aggressive.
- The future of internet adoption—and by extension, streaming—was highly uncertain.

Every move Netflix made carried existential risk:

- If DVDs didn't catch on, the company would collapse.
- If Blockbuster crushed them more quickly, they would disappear.
- If funding dried up, it would be over.

This is how each of the cofounders described it.

"There were so many times when it felt like it would all fall apart. We were running out of cash. We were guessing about the future." – *Reed Hastings*

"Everything was working against us: the technology, the logistics, the economics. It was constant chaos." – *Marc Randolph*

To survive, Netflix relied on relentless adjustment—pivoting from DVD sales to rentals to a subscription model—along with operational discipline, perfecting its inventory and delivery logistics. Above all, Netflix endured massive uncertainty, including surviving the dot-com crash that wiped out countless start-ups.

Netflix succeeded not because the market was fair or predictable, but because it navigated the cruel sea with greater resilience, agility, and endurance than its competitors.

Key Takeaways

When you operate in a cruel sea (harsh market, brutal start-up environment, volatile economy):

- Stop wishing for fairness.
- Be adaptive and build adaptive systems.
- Train for toughness.
- Expect hardship—and plan to win through endurance.

How to Apply the Cruel Sea Mental Model

1. Accept that the market and business in general are indifferent. Success is not a result of your good intentions, passion, or early effort.

- Customers can leave without warning.
- Competitors can crush you without mercy.
- Crises can wipe out years of work.

So you need a mindset shift: stop expecting fairness. Build for resilience, not sympathy.

2. Prepare for constant, grinding pressure.

The sailors faced endless fatigue, terror, and stress—with no guaranteed reward.

Business application: In modern business, chronic challenges (supply chain disruptions, employee turnover, regulatory shifts) are the *normal waves*, not exceptions.

Mindset shift: Set structures (processes, culture, cash reserves) to assume constant adversity, not perfectly smooth sailing.

3. Make tough, imperfect decisions with speed.

Captain Ericson had to make decisions and some of them quickly. Most of the time, he didn't have enough information or enough time. He relied on the mental models in his head to make judgments quickly.

Related Frameworks

- Using the **Franklin Framework** is a way to keep moving, even when things go wrong.
- Sometimes you just need to see the big picture to better assess your successes and setbacks. The **Zoom In/Zoom Out Move** looks at the problem from micro to macro and back.
- Using the **Six Honest Serving Men** model to focus on the facts may help ground you with the cruel sea.

"You can't control the sea, but you can control your ship."
– *Adapted from US Navy leadership principles*

Chapter 38
So What, Now What?

There are moments everyone faces—when the data is murky, the pressure is high, and the clock is ticking. No one is telling you what the right decisions is. Endless Googling won't help. All you'll have is how you think.

That's when mental models stop being academic. They become your lifeline.

Throughout this book, you've encountered dozens of powerful ways to think more clearly, frame problems more effectively, and move through uncertainty with confidence. From First Principles Thinking to the OODA Loop, from Inversion to the Stockdale Paradox, each model you've explored adds another tool to your mental toolkit.

But here's the most important lesson: It's not about mastering all of them. It's about building your own latticework—a small set of versatile, high-leverage models you can call on instinctively.

Charlie Munger wasn't great because he memorized hundreds of models. He was great because he knew when to apply the right ones, and how to mix them. Harold Hook didn't map systems for sport—he did it to lead people with clarity and foresight. The best decision-makers aren't just intelligent; they are disciplined thinkers who have trained themselves to pause, frame, and reflect before acting.

Mental models are not a magic bullet. They won't eliminate failure. But they do something better: they reduce avoidable failure. They make you more aware of the assumptions, biases, and blind spots that lead others off-course. They help you ask better questions, see second-order effects, and know when to act—or wait.

Building Your Own Latticework

As you close this book, consider a few next steps:

- Choose your top five models—the ones that lit up your thinking—and revisit them often. Commit them to muscle memory.
- Pair models together. Use probabilistic thinking with Bayesian Learning, or Circle of Control with Scenario Planning. Great thinkers stack models for strength.
- Teach them. The best way to solidify a mental model is to use it in conversation, decision meetings, and mentoring. If you can explain it simply, you own it.
- Create a mental dashboard. Before major decisions, ask yourself: "What models am I using to interpret this? What am I missing?"

Final Thoughts: Decision-Making as Craft

Decision-making is not a talent—it's a craft. Like any craft, it sharpens with practice, feedback, and the right tools. That's what this book was meant to give you: a better set of tools, drawn from history, psychology, strategy, and the trenches of real business.

When I founded Experience to Lead, I wanted to help leaders see with new eyes. Mental models have been the backbone of that work—from the boardrooms of Fortune 500 companies to the conversations that change lives one decision at a time. They've helped me, and I hope they'll help you too.

You won't always get it right. But with strong models, you'll get it right more often. And when the pressure's on, that can make all the difference.

My father used to tease me by saying, "If you're faced with a tough decision, just think what a smart boy would do. Then copy him." Those smart people, like Charlie Munger, Oprah Winfrey, and Jeff Bezos, use mental models. That's **How Smart People Think.**

Alphabetical Listing of Mental Models in this Book

Anchoring Bias: The tendency to give disproportionate weight to the first information received when making judgments or decisions.

Anti-Fragility: A system's ability to thrive and grow stronger in response to stress, volatility, or disruption.

Attribution Error: The bias of overemphasizing personal traits and underestimating situational factors in explaining others' behavior.

Bayesian Learning: A method of updating beliefs or probabilities based on new evidence using Bayes' theorem.

Bezos's Two-way Doors: A decision-making concept distinguishing between reversible ("two-way") and irreversible ("one-way") choices.

Circle of Control: A model that focuses attention on what you can directly influence, rather than worrying about what you cannot.

Confirmation Bias: The tendency to seek, interpret, and remember information that supports existing beliefs.

Cruel Sea: A metaphor for the fact that while you may make your best decision every time, the results will vary because of factors beyond your control.

Divergent and Convergent Thinking: Divergent thinking generates many creative options, while convergent thinking narrows them to the best choice.

Dr. Phil: The television personality often asks two questions: "What were you thinking when you did that?" and "How did that work out for you?" These questions are a version of reflective accountability to take responsibility for your actions.

Eisenhower Matrix: A time-management tool that categorizes tasks by urgency and importance to prioritize actions.

Expected Value: The weighted average outcome of a decision, factoring in probabilities and payoffs.

Fast and Slow Thinking: Daniel Kahneman's framework contrasts intuitive, quick System 1 thinking with deliberate, logical System 2 thinking.

First Principles Thinking: A problem-solving approach that breaks issues down to their fundamental truths and builds up solutions from there.

Franklin Framework: A structured method of self-improvement and productivity inspired by Benjamin Franklin's daily planning and virtues system.

Goal Shedding: The deliberate act of discarding goals that no longer serve purpose or alignment.

Inversion: A mental model of approaching problems by considering the opposite outcome or how to avoid failure.

Latticework of Models: Charlie Munger's idea that decision-making is strongest when built on a network of diverse mental models.

Loss Aversion: The bias where people feel losses more intensely than equivalent gains.

Map vs. Territory: The distinction between representations of reality (maps, models) and reality itself (the territory).

Marshmallows: A reference to the "marshmallow test" on delayed gratification and self-control.

Minimum Commitment: A strategy of testing ideas with the least amount of resources, effort, or time before scaling.

No-cost Consultant: The concept of informally learning from others' experiences, insights, or mistakes without paying a price yourself.

Occam's Razor: The principle that the simplest explanation, with the fewest assumptions, is often the best.

OODA Loop: A decision-making cycle of Observe, Orient, Decide, Act used for adaptability in fast-changing situations.

Opportunity Cost: The value of the next-best alternative you give up when making a decision.

Pareto Principle: The idea that 80% of outcomes often stem from 20% of causes.

Probabilistic Thinking: Making decisions by weighing the likelihood of different outcomes rather than relying on certainty.

Say Three, Pick One: A decision technique used by Navy SEALs of generating three options before selecting the best one.

Scenario Planning: A strategic method of preparing for multiple plausible futures by imagining varied scenarios.

Second-Order Thinking: Considering not just immediate effects but also the longer-term and indirect consequences of decisions.

Self-efficacy: A person's belief in their own ability to succeed at specific tasks or challenges.

Six Honest Serving Men: Kipling's framework of asking "What, Why, When, How, Where, and Who" to understand and solve problems.

Stockdale Paradox: Balancing unwavering faith in eventual success with the discipline to confront brutal present realities.

Sunk Cost: Resources already spent that should not factor into future decisions but often bias judgment.

Tame and Wicked Problems: Tame problems have clear solutions, while wicked problems are complex, ambiguous, and resistant to resolution.

Zooming In and Out: A thinking skill of shifting between detailed (micro) and big-picture (macro) perspectives for better insight.

Expand Your Thinking: Additional Resources

To enrich your journey through this book's ideas, we've curated exclusive resources designed to deepen your understanding and broaden your perspective.

Mind Map: The Book's Mental Model

Scan the QR code to explore a visual map that distills the core mental frameworks presented throughout the book. It's perfect for grasping connections, revisiting key insights, and triggering new interpretations.

Further Reading & Literary References

Want to take your learning even further? This QR code connects you to a selection of thought-provoking articles, book recommendations, and academic sources to guide your extended study—whether you're a curious beginner or a lifelong learner.

These tools are here to support your intellectual growth. Scan them, save them, share them and make them yours.

www.ingramcontent.com/pod-product-compliance
Lightning Source LLC
Chambersburg PA
CBHW071204210326
41597CB00016B/1664

9798886360615